TWO WHEELS DOWN

THE STORY OF ONE MAN, HIS MOTORCYCLE, AND LIFE ON THE ROAD

TWO WHEELS DOWN

THE STORY OF ONE MAN, HIS MOTORCYCLE, AND LIFE ON THE ROAD

C.R. BONEY

Copyrighted Material

Two Wheels Down: A Tale of One Man, His Motorcycle, and Life on the Road

Copyright © 2019 by Christopher R. Boney/C.R. Boney's Creative Works

All Rights Reserved.

No part of this publication may be reproduced, stored in a retrieval system or transmitted, in any form or by any means—electronic, mechanical, photocopying, recording or otherwise—without prior written permission from the publisher, except for the inclusion of brief quotations in a review.

For information about this title or to order other books and/or electronic media, contact the publisher:

C.R. Boney's Creative Works
P.O. Box 6907
Great Falls, MT 59406
crboney2@gmail.com

Library of Congress Control Number: 2018911108

Isbns:
978-1-7326325-0-9 (print)
978-1-7326325-1-6 (eBook)

Printed in the United States of America

Cover and Interior design: 1106 Design

Publisher's Cataloging-In-Publication Data
(Prepared by The Donohue Group, Inc.)

Names: Boney, C. R. (Christopher R.), author.
Title: Two wheels down : a tale of one man, his motorcycle, and life on the road / C.R. Boney.
Description: Great Falls, MT : C.R. Boney's Creative Works, [2018]
Identifiers: ISBN 9781732632509 (print) | ISBN 9781732632516 (ebook)
Subjects: LCSH: Boney, C. R. (Christopher R.)--Travel--Europe. | Motorcyclists--Biography. | Motorcycling--Europe. | Self-actualization (Psychology) | LCGFT: Travel writing. | Diaries. | Autobiographies.
Classification: LCC G226.B66 A3 2018 (print) | LCC G226.B66 (ebook) | DDC 910.4092--dc23

CONTENTS

DEDICATIONS vii

THANK-YOUS ix

PROLOGUE 1
   A Little Bit About Me 1
   Why I Ride 4
   The Real Star 11
   The Goals 16
   It Is What It Is 18

MALMÖ 19
   Chapter 1: Preparations 21
   Chapter 2: Home—Malmö 31
   Chapter 3: Malmö—Home 47

RIDE THE ALPS 65
Chapter 4: Home—Spangdahlem Air Base . . 67
Chapter 5: Spangdahlem Air Base—
   Garmisch 77
Chapter 6: My Own Poker Run 95
Chapter 7: Garmisch—Home 115

THE BIG TRIP 125
Chapter 8: Preparations 127
Chapter 9: Home—Gorlitz 135
Chapter 10: Gorlitz—Zagreb 145
Chapter 11: Zagreb—San Marino . . . 167
Chapter 12: San Marino—Lörrach . . . 181
Chapter 13: Lörrach—Home 199

THE WINTER RIDE 215
Chapter 14: Preparations 217
Chapter 15: Home—Wales 225
Chapter 16: Wales—Home 251

EPILOGUE 267
Epilogue 269
Life After the Rides 269
Marriage 270
Job and Transition 272
Life 279

About the Author 283

DEDICATIONS

TO MY WIFE

First and foremost, this book is dedicated to my wife, Glorianna. Our relationship was tested time and again while I worked on my writing. We came close so many times to calling it quits and walking away from our marriage. And while I can't see into the future, I know that, because we walked through the fire together, you are much stronger, I am much stronger, and WE are much stronger for it. Thank you for being my partner on this crazy ride, and may we have many more crazy rides together. I LOVE YOU!

TO MY PARENTS

I am truly blessed to have incredible beings such as both of you in my life. I am the man I am today because of you. The hard lessons you taught me and real-life examples you provided guided me on my path to adulthood. You are truly incredible role models, and I appreciate you both. During this transition period, you've helped us not only physically (money, a free place to stay, networking connections, food, and so on) but also emotionally and spiritually. I've struggled in the past to ask for help, but when I did come calling, you welcomed us without hesitation, reservation, or judgment. I could never say enough or do enough to show the depths of my gratitude, so instead, I'll just say: I LOVE YOU!

TO THOSE WHO HAVE HELPED

When you are facing a true crisis in life, and if you open yourself to the possibility that people want to help, you will find that people truly do want to help. There are so many people to thank for their guidance, mentorship, action, help, a shoulder to cry on, and so forth. From friends to strangers, this road was made so much easier and safer thanks to you all. It's an incredible thing when the human spirit reaches beyond itself to lift someone else in need. People I'd never met called in all kinds of favors on my behalf for no other reason than that I needed their help. Please know that my life is amazing today because of each and every one of you who stepped up to help me when I needed it. THANK YOU!

THANK-YOUS

Thank you to:

Editors (alphabetical order):

- Nancy Desilets (WriteOnTrack.com)
- Audra Gorgiev (EditorExtraordinaire.com)

Design:
- 1106 Design Team (1106design.com)

PROLOGUE
A LITTLE BIT ABOUT ME

I was born to military parents in California, which, if you are hip to that life, you know it means moving around—a lot. My parents called it quits when I was about three years old, and so I moved around with my mom until she decided to leave the military and move back to Detroit, Michigan, to help my grandfather with his business. I spent most of my childhood in the inner city of Detroit, brought up by a single mother who was terrified that I would get caught up in some of the dangerous elements around us.

Growing up, I bounced back and forth between my mother and my father, spending most of my childhood years with my mother. I did enjoy a significant amount of time with my father as well, but he mostly had me during my brooding teen years. My father lived wanting nothing more in life than to raise his only son, and he lived for those times that we managed to spend together during my childhood.

Living between my parents meant I changed schools ten times from kindergarten to grade 12. Both of my parents endured struggles, living a life for which they scratched, cried, and bled. From my mom, I learned what it meant to conquer the daily grind, how to think critically, how to be independent, and how to adapt to the evolving and ever-changing landscape of life. Dad taught me compassion and the art of using patience to work for me, and provided an amazing blueprint for what makes a great husband and father. Between the two of them, I turned out alright, or at least that's what they'd have you believe—but, that's a story for another day.

I'm passionate about many things in life, including family, traveling, education, fencing (stabby-stabby; not buildy-buildy), my motorcycle, and writing. I am married to a wonderful woman, and while we don't have children right now, we both look forward to bringing new life into this world.

Traveling and adventuring is as necessary for me as breathing. I've been to all seven continents, more

PROLOGUE ★

than 60 different countries, crossed both the Arctic and Antarctic circles, summited one of the tallest mountains in the world, and so much more. In all my travels, I've experienced so many crazy adventures that I have material to write about for years to come.

This book is about my passion for riding, so you'll read all about that. In addition to my riding adventures, I place a lot of value on education—both formal and experiential—and have used both forms over the course of my career to bring great success to the people and organizations around me.

Formally, I received an MS and a PhD in Industrial/Organizational Psychology while serving in the U.S. Air Force. While in college, I began fencing in 2003 and haven't stopped since—competing in high-level tournaments all over the United States, as well as The Netherlands, Germany, and Belgium. I've also instructed, coached, and run my own fencing club. And, I've long desired to write and have my works published for the masses to read.

Aside from the dissertation I wrote, I have yet to venture into the realm of "author-hood." This is my first foray, and I am beyond elated. I'm really excited to step into the world of fiction and felt that this book could be a great first stab (no pun intended) at introducing myself to the literary world. Summing my education and interests provides a quick-and-dirty synopsis of the many passions that drive me to be the man I am today. This book, this new adventure, is about my experiences viewed through the lens of a combined passion for travel and motorcycle riding. Beginning in 2010 with my three-week trip to Tanzania and Zanzibar, I began to keep travel journals, detailing each day and each experience along my journey. Since then, I've accumulated many journals—pages filled with adventure, excitement, danger, sorrow, and most of all, a slice of real and unabashed life. This book is a detailed accounting of four particular motorcycle trips across the European continent over the span of about seven months. More than a just summary about my adventures, though, it is a heartfelt recollection of my life experiences during these adventures.

WHY I RIDE

I began riding in 2009 in Minot, North Dakota. Stationed in the state's frozen north, I decided to open a new chapter in my life, this time involving two wheels on the ground. After finding a great deal on a (comfortable and affordable) 2006 Honda VTX 1300, fully decked out with all the bells and whistles (including jumbo-sized saddlebags, a windshield, footboards, and aftermarket seats), I instantly loved my

PROLOGUE ★

new life on the road—exploring the northern plains with the roar of my engine, the threat of impending horrible pain and death subtly hovering at the edge of my consciousness, and the freedom of the open road under the clear blue skies.

Soon after I started riding, I also began reading Robert M. Pirsig's book *Zen and the Art of Motorcycle Maintenance*. That book truly had an impact in that I learned about the power of unhindered contemplation afforded by the freedom of being on the open road. If you are a motorcycle enthusiast or just love a good book, I encourage you to read his book (after you finish reading this book, of course).

I began riding with Konrad, a good friend of mine. We took the Motorcycle Safety Foundation's Basic Rider's Course together and both fell in love with riding. We practiced by taking rides to various small towns in North Dakota. In fact, the first long ride we took was to a pizzeria in a town called Bottineu. I opted for a full-face helmet (as I wanted to ensure my perfect chin would stay, well, perfect); he opted for a half-helmet and goggles, which exposed his face to the elements. He also rode without a windshield, whereas my used bike came with all the fixings, including a windshield.

After about 30 minutes on the road, we got to a four-way stop where we needed to turn right, and

Konrad decided to pull off to the side of the road. I assumed he was sore and wanted to stop and stretch, but when I stopped and walked over to him, I saw his reason for pulling over. His face was blackened with the carcasses of dead bugs that pelted him all the way from Minot. He opened his mouth to talk and, instead, spat out more bugs—his teeth their final resting place. I couldn't stop laughing, particularly because I had warned him against wearing the half-helmet (though, like him, I hadn't accounted for all the spring bugs). He pulled off his goggles, wiped his face, and then we continued on to our destination in anticipation of hot pizza and a cold beer. This time, though, we rode a little slower in an effort to spare his face from the sting of pelting bugs.

Konrad and I also started a small riding club with some fellow riders from work. Every month we'd choose a restaurant in a new small town about 35–45 minutes away from Minot. These planned outings attracted a fair number of riders—when we'd get to our destination, the food, beer, and camaraderie of a group of motorcycle enthusiasts were all such an intoxicating feeling. The restaurants enjoyed our business, and the sight of a long row of bikes lined up outside was a sight to behold in towns where not much really happened but the comings and goings of local farmers.

PROLOGUE ✯

Of our riding group, Konrad seemed to be the only one who shared my sense of adventure and the drive to push further down the road; thus, we made plans to go to the world-famous Sturgis Motorcycle Rally in South Dakota. We booked our spots at the Buffalo Chip campground, we shopped for the gear we'd need to set up a compact campsite, and we continued to practice riding. We did a dry run to build our riding stamina by biking to Wolf's Point, Montana. Why Wolf's Point? Simple—I have a fond affinity for wolves (and, I saw it on the map). In hindsight, I could've probably chosen a more scenic place to make our practice run. But we made it there and back with no issues, so we knew we were ready for the big one.

About three weeks before we were to leave for Sturgis, I got into a motorcycle accident. I was in the process of passing a vehicle on the left-hand side, going about 35 mph. The driver didn't see me, so she began changing lanes. Time seemed to slow down right at that moment. I quickly had to consider two options: roll back on the throttle and get in front of her before she clips my back tire, or hit the brakes and slide back behind her before she clips my front tire. I chose the latter, hitting both sets of brakes, sending my bike into a skid. My tires slipped from under me, and the bike slammed down on its side, skidding about 15 feet down the road. As I hit the pavement, my head slammed onto the concrete, making a loud cracking sound. I slid on the ground a short ways before popping up—adrenaline pumping, and absolutely furious.

I was so angry that I needed a minute to cool off before approaching the car to speak with the young lady behind the wheel. Why was I so angry? After all, life happens, right? With my bike wrecked so close to my Sturgis trip, I was upset because I wasn't sure I'd be able to get it fixed in time. All of the preparation, planning, and excitement was now in jeopardy because some driver had not been paying attention.

Luckily, she admitted fault, and her insurance was quick to pay out, just in time to get my bike all fixed up. I took the opportunity to add much-needed gear on my bike—it looked brand-spanking new. With about a week to spare, all the preparations were complete and ready for the big trip.

The ride to Sturgis was my first truly big motorcycle trip—Konrad and I had a blast during the seven (turned six)–day trip. We rode through the famous Badlands in South Dakota and made it to Sturgis after riding about seven hours. During our week-long stay at Sturgis, among other attractions, we rode to the Mount Rushmore and Crazy Horse monuments, Devils Tower in Wyoming, the town of Deadwood—and

PROLOGUE ✯

the gravity-defying Cosmos Mystery Area near Rapid City, South Dakota. We took in an Aerosmith concert, watched an incredible motorcycle stunt show, visited the world-famous motorbike show, joined in with the parade of bikes down Sturgis's main strip, bar-hopped, and partied till the wee hours of the morning at the RV park where we camped. (More explicit detail of those events won't be shared, but they were memorable, to say the least.)

It turned out we had to cut short our week-long trip by a day—after day five of sightseeing on the road, we returned to a scene of muddy destruction at our campground. While we were gone, a massive hailstorm had ripped through the area, shredding tents and RVs, pock-marking bikes with dents—and even injuring some rally-goers. One guy was knocked unconscious by a golf-ball-sized chunk of hail.

When we got to our tents, Konrad's was shredded; everything inside was caked in mud, including some of his electronics. Astonishingly, my tent was still standing—nothing damaged. So the two of us had to huddle up in my now "two-man" tent for the night, and, needless to say, we decided that sharing such a tiny space for one night was more than enough. So, the next day—a day earlier than planned—we packed up, went down to the rally to enjoy some breakfast and do some last-minute souvenir shopping before hitting the road for home.

The Sturgis ride was truly one of the best road trips I've ever taken, made more memorable by Konrad's company and the fact that it was my very first long road trip on the bike. Those six days ignited my everlasting passion for riding.

If you're not a rider and you'd like a glimpse as to why I feel so strongly about riding, take a moment to try this exercise. Close your eyes and imagine that you are a sleek falcon. Being this falcon, you're soaring high in the sky with nothing but sunshine, puffy white clouds around you, and the land far below. You know that you can go as high, as fast, and as far as you could possibly want; you're a being with no limitations. If you could imagine yourself as that soaring falcon, imagine the pure joy and freedom you would experience. And, if you can imagine being a falcon, then you can begin to understand why motorcycle riding is such a thrill and a passion for so many people. I've never felt freer in my life than when I'm riding my bike on the open road. That feeling ignited within me when my buddy and I went on the Sturgis trip. This introduction, describing how I fell—hook, line, and sinker—for riding, provides an appropriate perspective for and the basis on which I wrote this book. Sometimes I interject events happening in my life that are not related to the ride itself. Understand that the freedom I experience while on the back of my bike also lends itself to contemplating my life in all of its brutal honesty.

THE REAL STAR

The one constant in this book is also the real star of the show—my motorcycle, affectionately called the Knargly Bastard (KB), named after my circle of friends from my earlier days in Belgium. KB is a 2013 Harley Davidson 110th Anniversary Edition Fat Boy Lo, and "he" and I met in early June of 2014.

Although stationed in Belgium, I was at the U.S. Ramstein Air Base in Germany for a time, undergoing training for my new job. After class, I wandered over to the Base Exchange (which, at this particular base, is an actual shopping mall, unlike other retail base exchanges). I spied a Harley Davidson dealership—so, in I walked. Before arriving in Belgium, I had been thinking about upgrading my bike to a Harley Davidson. I wanted more power, and I really liked the H-D community.

As I walked around the store looking at the bikes, my eyes landed on one in particular. It had a unique paint scheme—mainly black and brown with red and gold pin-striping accents. All of the accessories and accents were black, and the bike had a very rugged look to it. I thought to myself, "This would be my style of bike—if I were to get one." As I began to walk away, the salesman lazily called out, "That's a special-edition bike, only so many of them made. It has the serial number on the plate by the gauge." He didn't strike me as being particularly knowledgeable about the bike; he didn't even know the model. But I didn't really care; I wasn't seriously looking to buy right then, anyways. Some people at work were pushing hard to convince me to buy a BMW 1200 GS. They swore by the BMW, and even stopped riding their Harleys in favor of the adventurer-style bike. I had planned to test both styles out before seriously deciding which to buy.

Back to the bike at hand: after the salesman suggested I look at the serial-number plate, I came back and leaned over the bike, looking for the number. My eyes landed on it—Vehicle Number: 1002/1750. At that moment, the world around me froze, and I could feel my heart skip a beat in my chest. I had to do a double-take, because there was no way in hell the number on this bike could be 1002. But, there it was, clear as day. This bike was placed here especially for me to stumble across, no doubt about it.

Okay, you're probably wondering why 1002 is such a significant number for me. First, it's my day of birth,

PROLOGUE ✮

October 2 (1002), my favorite day of the year. Second, it is a number that I seem to always see everywhere I go. I could randomly check the time, and it will be flashing 10:02.

I first became aware of my connection to this 1002 number in high school after a few seemingly insignificant instances where it caught my attention. In college, I chose a room in an empty four-bedroom apartment and then happened to look out the window. The apartment right across from me? Yep, you guessed it: 1002.

There are so many more examples than I can remember, but this number became a superstitious guide. Anytime I saw it, I had a strong feeling I was somehow, some way, on the right path. To the nonbelievers, go ahead and roll your eyes—hell, I don't blame you—but I can tell you that following my gut whenever I come across the number 1002 has yet to burn me. Maybe one day it will (and all my memories were simply coincidences), but I'm not holding my breath. So, now you can understand why eyeballing that number, 1002, on a random bike in a random store in Europe, after deciding to upgrade my bike, is one too many coincidences to ignore.

Not one for expensive impulse purchases, I decided to sleep on it before making a decision. When I got to my hotel room, I called my wife, Glo, told her what had happened, and asked for her opinion on the matter. Ever the enabler, she said, "Baby, go for it!" Armed with a positive response from the missus, I strengthened my resolve to take the plunge and purchase the bike. During lunch break that following day, I made my way back to the store. I could feel it in my soul that it was meant to be and that this particular bike was to be mine.

I walked through the doors, full of confidence and swagger—everything about my demeanor spoke to my intention as I approached the sales representative, Bronaugh. I pointed to my soon-to-be bike and said, "I would like to buy that bike, the 2013 110th Anniversary Fat Boy Lo." Bronaugh praised my selection and told me how good my taste was (yeah, typical sales tactics). But then, what she said next absolutely rocked my world: "This bike is actually already reserved, plus there's another person in front of you for that bike. So, you are third in line." I felt betrayed. How could this bike be here in front of me and not be mine? Deflated, I explained the importance of the serial number, and she sympathized. She offered to show me other, newer bikes, but I was set—it was either that bike or nothing at all. I added my name to the expanding list of hopeful buyers and left the store, head hung low.

Later the next day, Bronaugh called me: "Hey, just wanted to let you know that the guy with the deposit

PROLOGUE ✯

unreserved the bike! Only one other person in front of you for the bike." I tempered my excitement; after all, the next buyer in line could be just as serious about purchasing the bike as I was.

The following day, I called Bronaugh at the shop and asked about the guy on the list ahead of me. She explained that he had a certain number of days that he could have the bike on hold before she could offer it to the next guy on the list—me. I had to tell her I'd be gone by then (back to my base), to which she replied, "Let me see what I can do—I'll call you back."

The next day, she did call me back: "The bike is all yours, if you still want it!" I was shocked! She explained that she didn't know why the first person backed out, but she'd convinced the next guy (the buyer ahead of me) to purchase a different, newer bike, and cut him a sweet deal on it. (As it turned out, apparently his wife liked the Fat Boy Lo bike more than he did.)

So, batter up, baby! I went straight to the dealership during lunch and put my money down on the Harley. After class that afternoon, I went back to the store to finish the paperwork and pose for some pictures next to *my* new bike. Bronaugh said that the bike was a year old and had been reserved more than seven times since it hit the showroom floor—but that no one had followed through on buying it. We joked that it was just waiting—waiting for me—to come pick it up; but there's always some truth in jest. I now have no doubt that this Harley was truly meant for me, superstitious nonsense and all (I sense some eye-rolling going on). And with that, the bike was mine! I honestly believe this bike was custom-made for me and was placed in my life path—there were too many "coincidences" that added up for it to be just chance. I get chills every time I think about how I came to possess KB. And now that you know the backstory of KB, the star of this book, let's talk expectations.

THE GOALS

My life is a collection of completed and unfinished goals of all shapes and sizes. I've written specifically about two of my travel goals that I was chasing while living in Belgium. First, I set a goal to hit every European country while stationed in Belgium. I used any and every means at my disposal—be it by train, motorcycle, car, plane, boat—whatever. I was determined to touch all of Europe. This goal was sparked from my competitive spirit.

When I arrived at my duty station in Belgium in May of 2014, I was greeted by my second-in-command, Bobby, and he quickly made sure I *knew* he was *the* most well-traveled individual at the base. With my extensive

PROLOGUE ✪

experience traveling the world (such as hitting all seven continents by the age of 30, backpacking across South America, ice caving in the Arctic, and so on), I humored him for a bit with awe and attentiveness. Then when I finally revealed my detailed travel resume, his comeback was, "Well, you can have the world; I am crushing you in Europe."

That stirred up the competitive raging fire and boiling testosterone from within, so I threw down the gauntlet and issued a challenge. I told him that before I left Belgium, I was going to travel to far more European countries than he will have. Not only that, the only reason we would end up in a tie would be because we both traveled to all of them. So, unless he traveled to every country in Europe, he was destined to lose.

He accepted the challenge—and with that, the game was on! We drew up a list of countries that would count toward completing the challenge. At that point in 2014, I was about nine European countries behind his total. Fast-forward to today: I have decimated that list, setting foot in every country on the list. He unofficially bowed out from completing our competition in 2015, when his son was born, so it was all but over—but I was still determined to hit all the countries we agreed to.

My second travel goal became what is the central theme of this book and, at times, the theme is also a slice of my life. I was determined to ride KB through 20 European countries. As the story unfolds, my travel goal was initially 10 countries, but I soon ratcheted it up a notch to what had become my journey (20 countries) and, subsequently, this book. It was a challenge I issued to myself—I wanted to explore Europe on my bike—and this personal test provided the motivation to really see the nooks and crannies of the continent. It was surprising how quickly the goal became my focus—and my salvation.

IT IS WHAT IT IS

This book is about real life. Not all life happens the way we would like or expect, but whatever does happen is real, just the way we experience it. It was created by my collection of motorcycle diary entries from June 2016 to January 2017. The book is sometimes candid and always authentic—a genuine look at life as seen through my eyes during the span of seven months. I am excited to let you into my world, even if it is only a small snapshot. It is my hope that you open yourself to the reality of your own life through the lens with which you will view my life and circumstances during my adventures.

Grab your motorcycle, gear up, and ride with me on this journey. . . .

MALMÖ

Countries to Travel to:

★ Belgium (1 of 10)
★ The Netherlands (2 of 10)
★ Germany (3 of 10)
★ Denmark (4 of 10)
★ Sweden (5 of 10)

Miles/Kilometers Traveled: 1,138 mi/1,832 km

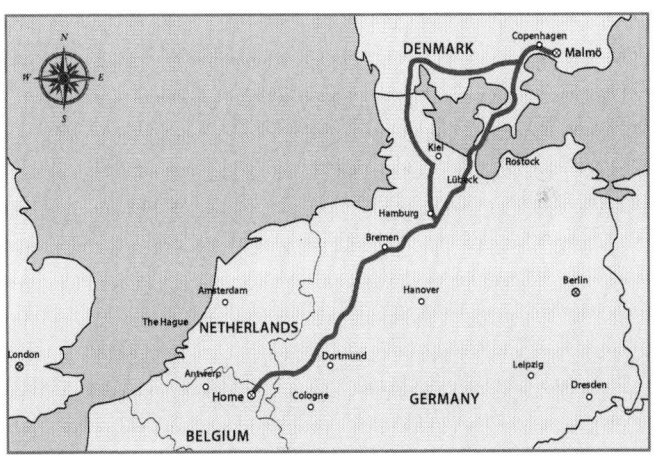

Chapter 1

PREPARATIONS
16 JUNE 2016

I've had my new Harley ("KB") for almost two years now and have barely put it on the road—I'm ashamed to have neglected it for so long. Well, this year I'm going to put some serious miles on it, because Glo and I are set to move back to the United States next May. I put a big trip, the annual "Ride the Alps," on my schedule for next weekend, but I wanted to flex my riding muscles. I didn't have a lot of riding experience, especially on long road trips. So, earlier this week I pulled up a map online and looked for someplace cool that I could knock out a round trip over a weekend. I finally settled on a trip to Malmö, Sweden. The weather forecast looked good, and it was only about a nine-hour ride. This trip would be my second-biggest trip—and the first by myself—in seven years, and I was incredibly nervous (and excited)!

I planned this ride as a test run because I'd committed to participating in the "Ride the Alps" trip at the Edelweiss Resort in southeastern Germany the following week. I needed to know what I could handle—just me and my bike—before getting on the road with other riders. I hadn't ridden a lot in a very long time, and I didn't want to bite off more of a trip than I could chew, nor did I want to be a hindrance during the trip as an inexperienced rider. I had no idea what to expect or how this trip would play out.

I knew I had the willpower to go the distance, but was there going to be a cost? I imagined I'd be exhausted and sore by the time I returned home. But worry and nerves aside, I felt the rush of the anticipation, the thrill—I was about to embark on a new adventure! The same anticipations that played on my nerves also fed my excitement—I'm a thrill-seeker, nothing too extreme—but a thrill-seeker nonetheless.

There is a level of exhilaration in diving into the unknown and swimming to the other side to see what you'll find. Will you find the jaws of a vicious monster just under the surface, ready to gobble you up? Or will you find a treasure so unique that only those brave enough to make the leap will be privy to its splendor? I've taken enough gambles and risks while traveling to know which category I fall under. I have traveled across the world, embarking on all kinds of unique adventures, dueling with the beasts of the unknown and not always finding treasure.

I often feel that I live my life as two beings—the resident and adventurer. The resident works, is married, makes plans, hosts board-game nights, and does other such life stuff. The adventurer, however, craves new and unique experiences. The adventurer seeks to conquer the world, engages in death-defying acts, and tells tales that need telling. I am both of these beings, but now it's time for the resident to rest and for the adventurer to boldly step forward!

Logistically, I was ready to roll. I bought a roll bag from the Harley-Davidson Fraussen dealership in Genk. It was a medium-sized bag with plenty of space for a solo mission. The bag also came with a rain cover for protection during inclement weather. The bag was a bit of a pain to get onto the bike's luggage rack, however. The mechanisms used to attach the bag were two very long straps that I had to wrap around the backrest supports, over and over again. It fastened with fairly heavy-duty ratchet fasteners, and then I rolled the extra strap length up nice and neat and used Velcro to secure it. (The retrofit effort was a small price to pay for all the benefits this bag offered.)

I also picked up a Garmin Zumo 395 GPS, which is specifically designed for motorcycles. This device was absolutely awesome! The most important features I needed to have included Bluetooth connectivity, a music player, remote controls for the Garmin action camera, and a motorcycle shop locator feature. One of the most unique features of the GPS, though, was a tire-pressure indicator. It required the purchase of two sensors, which I bought and installed on my tires. These sensors communicated with the GPS unit, and when the tire pressure was too low, it would send a signal to the GPS, which would alert me that I needed to add tire air. I hadn't even known such technology was available! There were also many other features on the GPS device that I didn't care about, at least at the time.

My other purchases included a brand-new Schubert helmet and a low-profile Bluetooth headset (a two-pack, one for me and one for Glo). The Schubert helmet was ridiculously expensive, but the cheaper helmets I owned didn't fit well with the addition of the headset. I also figured that if I was going to invest heavily into any one accessory, it should probably be something that would protect my brain matter.

PREPARATIONS ✭

I had amassed all kinds of new toys and gadgets to make this (and future trips) as fun as possible. I loaded in the European maps and put 32 gigabytes of music on the SD card in the GPS. The GPS also had a trip-plotter feature that I used to input all of my planned stops.

Finally, the "pièce de résistance" purchase for the trip was an Air Hawk R Sport seat cushion. It took me a while to locate one of these, and even then I didn't expect to find this particular model. The seat cushion had a rubber air bladder with an easy-to-use air valve. The concept was that air would act as the cushion, shifting with the rider as they shifted. It was also supposed to provide better support for the lower back and tailbone. I played with the air levels, adjusting it as I sat on the bike in the garage until the cushion felt comfortable, and then finished installing it on top of the stock seat. Eventually, I want to get a custom seat; however, this setup would have to do in the meantime.

I planned for a three-day/two-night trip (the worst-case scenario) but wanted to shoot for a two-day/one-night trip—the best case. My route would take me through Germany, by way of Hamburg, to a ferry that would take me to Denmark. Once on the other side of the Fehmarn Belt in the Baltic Sea (the strait that separates Germany and Denmark), I planned to ride up through Denmark to Copenhagen and across the Øresund Bridge to my final stop: Malmö, Sweden.

I found Harley Davidson dealerships to stop at along the way; I wanted to collect souvenirs (T-shirts, patches, and pins) from as many locations as I could. I was thrilled at the opportunity to ride my bike through so many different countries—so thrilled, in fact, that I decided then and there to create a "new" travel goal: I wanted to ride my bike through 10 European countries. The more I thought about the possibilities of future trips and adding to my collection of countries on the back of KB, the more excited and pumped I felt. This short weekend trip would put me five countries into this new goal of mine, the halfway point in two days! The following week's trip could potentially wrap up my new travel goal, making it arguably the easiest goal I've set for myself.

Aside from the excitement of crossing so many different countries on my bike, I was also really stoked to visit the Harley Davidson dealership in Copenhagen. I like Copenhagen—like it quite a bit. The last time I was there, Glo and I had met up with my childhood friend Angel and a good friend of hers for the start of a Baltic cruise we all took, which left from a seaport in Copenhagen. Glo and I arrived a few days early so we could explore the beautiful city.

PREPARATIONS ★

Two things in particular about Copenhagen stood out for me on this visit. First, many, many people were adorned with tattoos. Old and young alike seemed to thoroughly enjoy displaying various skin art. As a fan of tattoos myself, I enjoyed looking at all the artwork; it appeared that there were some talented tattoo artists in the area.

The second thing about Copenhagen that stood out was its layout. Although it was a very large city, everything about the way it was organized seemed to guide pedestrians toward the waterfront. It didn't matter which street we walked down, we always seemed to pop out closer to the waterfront, as if it there were a faint magnetic pull toward the water. It was very easy to navigate the city on foot, and it never took long to find beautiful views of the water or the city. I was excited to get back to Copenhagen on my bike and explore different areas.

When I'm traveling, there are only a few places that just give me a strong "Home" feeling. I don't feel it often, but when I do, I feel it immensely. While tooling around Copenhagen during the first visit, I got that "Home" feeling, and I began to envision a pretty great life there. Knowing how cold it got in the winters concerned me, and convincing Glo that this city had great potential could prove to be challenging. Surprisingly, after passing the idea on to her, she wasn't opposed to considering the possibility.

One thing I really appreciate about Glo is that she's just as set on retiring outside the U.S. as I was—we clashed only on where we would want it to be. I was in love with the idea of settling down in South America, especially Argentina or Brazil. She was more into the European scene. Honestly, I could do either continent with no problem, so we agreed that Europe was where we'd look to possibly take root before we hit retirement.

Packing for this trip was easy because I planned to bring only my riding jeans (which I swore had to have weighed the same as full plate mail the knights of old wore), a few T-shirts, and extra socks and underwear. I did bring a hoodie for layering purposes. I packed my work phone (which was like a burner phone you'd see on shows like the drug-dealing crime war series "The Wire"). I also packed a road map provided by Harley Davidson HOG (the Harley Owners Group). I wanted to make sure that if something happened to my GPS, I'd be good to go with my old-fashioned map skills and not miss a beat. I put my motorcycle registration paperwork and other important documents in a Ziploc bag and threw them into the swingarm bag attached to the bike behind my left leg. And with all that packed up and ready, my preparations were complete! I took comfort in knowing that if I needed anything while on the road, I would have the funds in the wallet and the space in the roll bag to accommodate it.

Glo seemed fairly disinterested overall in the trip, though I'm sure she (at a minimum) worried for my safety. It was only six months prior that our friend was in a brutal motorcycle crash from which he was still receiving reconstructive surgeries on his leg. I'm sure thoughts flowed through her mind quite a bit about what could happen, but she makes it a point to keep those thoughts to herself. She tells me all the time that I'm stubborn, so maybe she figured it wouldn't matter anyway if she voiced her concerns—I'd still do the trip. And, she wouldn't be wrong (for worrying, and about my stubbornness). Once I've dug my heels in the sand, determined to do something, there wasn't a lot that could happen that would deter me from my chosen path.

I wanted to get an early start, so after I did my final checks, ate dinner with Glo, and spent some extra time with her, I decided to call it an early night. With closed eyes, waiting for sleep to overtake me, I could feel the excitement building.

Chapter 2
HOME–MALMÖ
17 JUNE 2016

So, today's ride to Malmö, Sweden, is meant to flex my riding muscles and stamina prior to the "Ride the Alps" trip the following week. The projected weather for that trip was not looking good, and Glo had already bowed out because she didn't want to be miserable on the bike. But, today I put my trepidations about next week's trip aside and focused my determination on conquering this mountain before me.

I packed my bag and loaded up the bike last night. I got up this morning at about 0415 (4:15 AM using 12-hour clock notation) so that I could hit the road by

0500. I wanted to beat the rain at the start of the trip, to see if I could outrun it. I had already plotted all the major stops: the Harley Davidson store in Hamburg-Nord, Cap's Harley-Davidson in Copenhagen, and the ProBike Malmö shop in Malmö, Sweden.

I also found a nice hotel on the outskirts of Malmö to mark the halfway point of this journey. I looked for a place that had a parking garage so I didn't have to leave my bike out in the elements—both weather and crime. Harley Davidson motorcycles go for big money here in Europe, so I've been warned to be careful where I leave my bike—the threat of theft was apparently waiting around every corner.

I had no idea how this trip would turn out; I just knew I was determined to make good on the challenge. It was a lot to bite off—and by myself, nonetheless. As I putzed about—getting dressed, eating oatmeal, and gathering last-minute items for the road—I could feel my nerves starting to fire. I was nervous! If something were to happen, I'd be out there all alone. That thought was both chilling and exhilarating; I knew it was the thrill-seeker in my blood. I'm not sure what drives me to set challenges just so I can smash them, but the thought of knocking down challenges definitely gets my blood pumping.

With everything packed and ready, I said my goodbyes to Glo, the animals (dog and cat), and my

HOME–MALMÖ

home. Since my goal was to ride through ten European countries, I counted Belgium by default because it's my home; so, one down, nine to go! I struck out on the road of adventure, ready to see what it offered, alone and unafraid.

As I set out, the weather was good, and there was zero traffic. I had perfectly timed my departure! I was so excited to leave that I forgot to put on some jams (music). I hastily corrected that oversight, and on went the tunes in my headset as I cruised around the small towns, heading toward the highway. Before long, I was merging onto an empty highway, cruising enroute to Hamburg, Germany.

With my music jamming from my helmet's mounted earphones and the rumble of the engine between my legs, I was in a headspace that let me sort through the jumbled thoughts darting around inside my skull. It's one of my favorite things about riding: the flow of my stream of consciousness is as free as how I feel when I'm riding down the road. And, the music acts as a conduit for that stream. I learned while working through graduate school that music helps move my thoughts from my head onto the paper. Ever since that discovery, music has been a necessary staple for most of my activities.

After about an hour, I stopped at a large Shell gas station and rest stop to grab some fuel and take a stretch. The seat cushion I got was definitely helping, but I was still feeling the pressure point on my tailbone. I played with the inflation system a little, but I didn't want to mess it up and then be on the road with an overinflated seat. It was pretty sensitive, and after tweaking it slightly, I knew I wouldn't get a good feel for the adjusted seat until I was riding the bike. I already felt as if I were sitting a little too high up on the bike, something I wanted to alleviate (sitting too high could be dangerous).

On the road again, the weather continued to hold up quite nicely. The sky wasn't bright and sunny, but the sky wasn't threatening rain, either. After I settled back into my groove on the road and into my music, I began to let my mind wander.

In my life at the moment, the biggest issue was the fact that I'd been passed up for promotion to the rank of Major. My leadership couldn't really explain what happened; they seemed as surprised as I was. I mean, 92 percent of eligible Captains got promoted. So, the Selection Board was telling me that I was in the bottom 8 percent? I was crushed, shamed, and embarrassed. Later, I found out that I had a missing decoration on my record, so I was able to apply for a supplemental board who would meet at a later date to re-review my promotion. I also found that my promotion package (that went to the Selection Board) had what appeared to be some sort of correction marks on the main page, which is not normal. No one could explain anything about them to me, and I was told that my leadership did not want to pursue it.

I felt that this was such a weird and ambiguous situation; it warranted a deeper look. It was frustrating that someone above my station decided that the inexplicable events weren't worth pursuing, and it was at my expense—not receiving the promotion. If the marked-up promotion package made it to the Board, it was likely it received little-to-no attention—especially if they felt that my leadership didn't care enough about my progression to warrant careful attention to detail. There's no telling what the Board will and will not consider in a slightly unconventional situation. This week, the supplemental promotion board met to go over my promotion package, so hopefully I'd find out the results in a month or so. I was lucky enough to get approved to meet with this supplemental board, which essentially gives me a second chance to receive the promotion.

At the same time I was putting together my package for the supplemental promotion board, I had to create another promotion package for what the Air Force considered to be my "actual" second and final chance to promote. As an officer, you get only two chances for promotion; "Above the Zone" is the second and final time. And though there are sometimes exceptions to the rule, the second and final chance is the norm. The opportunity to promote during this phase is severely reduced compared to an individual's first time around. And without a special endorsement from the top leadership, it's almost impossible to be promoted.

I reached out to a lot of people in my career field to help me build my next promotion package, looking to make it as strong as I could. I was hoping to get that endorsement, and I expressed to my leadership that I needed it from them; although it wasn't theirs to give, they *could* carry my case up to the top on my behalf. They seemed to be in my corner, telling me I was easily ready for promotion. But, even as I was putting my name down to volunteer to lead every event before the close-out of my performance report (to be as visibly deserving of the promotion as possible), I was told by one of the top people in my leadership chain that those volunteer opportunities were being held for one of my peers (who was promoted), and they wanted to give him more of a competitive edge for a spot in a professional military educational program.

I was furious! Here I was, scrambling to figure out how to salvage my career, and they're worried about a guy who's already made it? It was at that point I realized

HOME–MALMÖ

I was on my own. I still volunteered for every event because I wanted to show that I hadn't been defeated by my situation, but it was at that point I lost faith that my leadership had my back. Hearing that I wasn't as important as someone who had already achieved was a huge blow to the gut. I knew that I'd worked really hard from the day I'd arrived at my station, but in a brand-new job position and as a new flight commander, I felt that my boss had never really acknowledged my growth. I didn't really care much, because I knew how hard I'd worked—until I was passed over for promotion.

Then I saw the light, and I understood how my situation was tenuous at best. After being told that I wouldn't have the opportunity to beef up my chances because they wanted to help out the "other" guy, I knew that, despite the comforting words, I was on my own. I was absolutely confident that I would promote after the supplemental promotion board's review. My record was clean, I'd never failed a physical fitness test, and I'd performed well over the years. So, I decided not to push back, as the next promotion board probably wouldn't even matter.

The ride through Belgium and The Netherlands was uneventful. I passed through The Netherlands in a blink of an eye. The country is very small, and the portion I passed through to get to Germany amounted to no more than a sliver on the map—45 minutes on the road. The time spent in the country didn't matter to me for the purpose of my goal, however, so I mentally checked off country number 2 of 10!

This trip wasn't the first time I'd ridden my bike to The Netherlands; I had taken a motorcycle safety training course at a Dutch base just across the border. This part of the country is very green but otherwise undistinguishable from the Belgian landscape. Further west and north, the landscape flattens out and is littered with small canals, streams, and villages. The Netherlands' coastal areas are particularly beautiful, especially in the summer months.

Before long, I found myself crossing the border into Germany (and into country number 3 of 10 toward my goal). The scenery didn't change, so I fell back into my music, clearing my mind of any substantial thought.

As I rode into the city of Hamburg, I was running low on fuel, and the sky was threatening to deliver a downpour. I finally found a gas station on the way to the Harley Davidson shop I wanted to stop at and pulled up under the covered awning above the gas pumps. As I replaced the gas nozzle and mounted the bike, the downpour hit. Big-city riding in the rain on a Friday is not an ideal situation.

Eventually, I made it to the Harley shop Hamburg-Nord. I was able to find covered parking, so I locked up the steering column and made my way inside the enormous dealership. The reception was fairly cool; all stares and not a single greeting or smile. I asked the associate behind the sales counter if I could put my helmet behind the counter while I shopped; begrudgingly, she agreed. I handed her my wet helmet and made my way to the sales floor.

I searched out a shirt for myself and my friend Konrad. This was a shirt I've owed him for years! When we started riding together, he'd bought me a Harley Davidson shirt, and I was supposed to buy him a Honda motorcycle shirt to match my first bike. That was seven years ago, and the debt still weighed on my shoulders, even if he had likely long forgotten. Once I send it off, debt paid! I also looked for a patch and/or pin for my vest. They didn't have any store patches in stock, so a pin it was. After I made my purchases, I grabbed my helmet from the counter and a coffee from the vending machine next to the register, and sat on the couch in front of the TV. I wanted to take a nice break after coming this far.

There were two German riders sitting nearby, conversing. I tried striking up a conversation, but they spoke very little English and seemed very disinterested in talking to me anyways. That's fair; I was a stranger, and a foreigner, so maybe it was a bit presumptive on my part to assume that Harley Davidson could bring us together in a motorcycle-related discourse. . . .

After about a half-hour relaxing, I left the store at about noon to get back on the road. I packed my purchases and cranked up the bike. Hamburg was about the halfway point for the trip, so I was making good time. I had a good chunk of the ride left, but I was feeling great, both physically and mentally.

Then the trip took a turn for the worse. In trying to leave the city, I hit solid bumper-to-bumper traffic in the still-falling rain. To top it off, I wasn't comfortable splitting lanes (maneuvering between lanes of traffic), so I sat amongst the crawling traffic, getting pelted by large raindrops. When other bikers would pass me, I'd try to lane-split, but my confidence just wasn't there, so I spent much of the afternoon sitting in the rain. The traffic cleared up eventually, but it took a long time to get through it all— one-and-a-half hours, to be exact. It continued to rain long after the traffic subsided, further slowing my progress.

After getting clear of the city traffic, I stopped to get some gas, food, warmth, and free Wi-Fi. After fueling up, I made my way to a restaurant. Finding an empty table, I sat down, peeled off my gloves, jacket, and hoodie, and draped them over the backs of a few chairs so that they could dry somewhat. It felt good to get that wet weight off my shoulders and relax a bit.

HOME – MALMÖ

I didn't own any rain gear, and it showed. Everything was dripping wet. My shoes had puddles in them, and my socks were soaked. I was very uncomfortable—to the point of miserable. I knew I'd need to look for rain gear soon, but here in Europe, that could soak up some serious cash.

The meal—schnitzel and potatoes—was hot and delicious, so I was in no rush to get back out to embrace the elements. I chatted with Glo on the phone for a bit while I sat in my wet clothes and ate. I gave her a rundown about my experiences up to that point, but she seemed more interested in getting back to whatever television show she was watching and less interested about my adventures. (I get it; it's not for everybody, right?)

I finished eating and slowly began putting on all my gear. The hoodie was still soaked, and I debated whether or not to put it in my bag. I didn't have my jacket liner, so if it got chilly on the ride, I'd probably really miss it. So, I put the hoodie back on and covered it with the drenched and heavy jacket. After zipping everything up, I began the battle with my new gloves. The gloves I bought when I purchased my other gear prior to this trip were very frustrating. Every time I pulled them off, the inserts would bunch up and I would have to fight to get my fingers into each hole. It would take minutes—MINUTES—to put on my gloves. Being wet made this glove-dance even more frustrating. Finally, geared up and well fed, I left the restaurant and put my mind back to the grindstone, hand to the throttle, and wheels to the road.

I got turned around at some point when leaving Hamburg, so my GPS had me go up through Denmark's mainland and then over to Malmö, all without the use of a ferry. The original route had me take the ferry at Puttgarden, which was a shorter route. The revised route really didn't add much time to the trip, just time on the bike, and that time was adding up pretty quickly.

Not too long after leaving the restaurant, I came to the border crossing into Denmark. Shortly after crossing, the stormy clouds began to clear away, and I started seeing sun and blue skies for the first time all day. Seeing the sun out and encapsulated in the blue skies reenergized me something fierce, and after stopping to gas up in country number 4 of 10 toward my goal, I hit the road with a new fury never before seen on a bike (on my bike, anyways)!

The sky continued to clear, and I reveled in the beautiful countryside scenery. Everything was lush green and very clean. After having dealt with traffic and rain, I rejoiced in the sunny open road and the accompanying open spaces.

As I rode through mainland Denmark, I crossed a massive bridge connecting the mainland to one of the larger Danish islands. While crossing the bridge, I could feel the force and whip of the wind as it cut across the bridge, forcing me at points to lean quite far to the right, just to keep from getting pushed into the barrier. But, I didn't care, because as wet and chilly as I was (and now, hungry), I couldn't help but swell with intense joy and peacefulness. This is what I yearned for on the road. All of my physical aches and pains and any mental anguish evaporated with the light of the sun and the rush of the road under the soles of my boots. This was freedom!

I stopped for gas one last time just outside of Copenhagen. I didn't want to take a chance and get stuck in traffic sweating over the risk of running dry. But the traffic was very light and the city not so big to ride through on the highway. In no time, I came to the famous Øresund Bridge—or should I say, tunnel? I thought I'd go right across the bridge as I had earlier, but instead of climbing higher in the sky, I began sinking into the earth! The bridge began as a tunnel on the Denmark side and eventually rose out from the ground before climbing upward.

I cranked back on the throttle, getting more and more excited knowing that I was so close to the hotel. I'd been on the road so long, I took great pleasure in drowning the tunnel with the sound of my roaring engine. (I have to say, I'm sure other motorists find it annoying when motorcyclists crank their throttle in enclosed spaces, but it is so awesome to hear the echo of my engine's roar bounce from wall to wall.)

Eventually, I popped out and on to the five-mile-long bridge and rode across. The view was spectacular. The sun was still lingering low in the sky, so I had full visibility of the beautiful bridge and the stunning Øresund Strait. The sun glistened off the huge metal spires of the bridge and off the visibly calm waters underneath. I specified "visibly" because if the wind I fought on the bridge was any indication, the water underneath was anything but calm. There were times when I felt really uncomfortable with how much I had to lean over into the wind, but the five miles flew by as I took in the view.

Exiting the bridge put me square in Malmö, Sweden—I'd made it to the destination town! I officially hit five countries on the bike, and all in one day! I was both excited and relieved to have arrived safely. But, as I was riding to the hotel, I ran into a problem. The exit I needed to take was closed, and I ended up going 'round the roundabouts about four times, trying to figure it out. I finally decided that I'd just pick a road and the GPS would eventually recalculate—and it worked. Finally, I arrived!

I pulled up to the front of the hotel and tenderly got off the bike. I checked in and followed the receptionist's

HOME–MALMÖ

instructions to get my bike in the garage. It was very clean, but more importantly, safe and secure. I lugged my bag up to the room and called Glo to let her know I made it. I didn't talk long—I was starving, exhausted, and chilly (although most of my clothes had air-dried in the sun and wind after crossing into Denmark). I made my way downstairs and ordered Swedish meatballs (I'd heard the Swedes were famous for their meatballs) and fries, and downed a Swedish beer while I waited for my food. I swear, that beer was the best I'd ever had, but I know it was the exhaustion and the high of accomplishment that likely made it taste so good.

I took my food upstairs, called Glo one last time to say goodnight, peeled off all my layers, took a steaming hot shower (it felt so good), and ate my dinner. I hung up all my clothes, hoping that when I headed out in the morning, they would be completely dry.

As I crawled into bed, my mind was still and serene from having proved to myself that I had what it takes to tough out a long, hard ride. I felt a swell of pride that I'd made it to this faraway land in a day, and I took that feeling with me to the land of slumber. Fifteen hours on the road will wipe anyone out, but not everyone can do it with a smile.

Chapter 3

MALMÖ–HOME
18 JUNE 2016

The hotel room bed felt so good! Because I had to wait for the ProBike motorcycle shop to open at 0900, I wasn't in a rush to get up. I hadn't set an alarm, but I woke up on my own pretty early. Surprisingly, I felt pretty good, considering how long and hard I'd ridden yesterday. I expected to wake up almost paralyzed with all-encompassing soreness.

As I lay in the comfortable Swedish bed, I considered how far I'd come in a day, as well as how far I was willing to go to accomplish what I'd set out to do. To say I am tenacious would be an understatement—once

I set my mind on achieving a goal, my nature is to not *just* achieve that goal but seek to blow the goal out of the water. I look for goals that are challenging, uncommon, and ones that I can feel supremely proud of completing.

Once I make up my mind, it takes a lot to move me from my path—sometimes, a detriment. Time spent on attaining my goals can sometimes compete with the time I put into my relationship with Glo. It's not as if she couldn't come along with me on my journey, but the emphasis is that it is MY journey, not our journey. I do make a point to seek out things we could accomplish together as well, but when it comes to living life, we have very different ways of enjoying it. We are very different people. I feel that I am adventurous, somewhat thrill-seeking, and willing to swim in the gray zone when it comes to rule-following; she enjoys the comfortable big-city life, is safety-minded, and is a very black-and-white follower of rules.

I'm not passing judgment on her way of enjoying life; it's just very different than mine, which can make enjoying life together more difficult. I know what I'm passionate about and what drives me forward every day, as well as the life I look forward to living once I've hit my career and investment goals. Because Glo is still finding herself in the world, she's more apt to being swept up into my plans and vision. That sometimes causes conflict between us; she sometimes feels more like a fixture in my life than a partner. Yet, I can't work with her on a joint vision if she hasn't figured out what she wants out of life. Regardless, I can feel the resentment and frustration she experiences at times, and while I feel for her, I'm not entirely sure what I can do about it. I look forward to the day I can support her in living out her dreams and working with her to build a dream life together. But while she discovers what she wants, I have some dreams of my own to live.

Eventually, I got out of bed and prepped my gear for the day's ride. After packing and getting dressed, I relaxed just a little more before lugging my gear downstairs to check out. I turned in my room cards at the reception desk and made my way toward the breakfast buffet to load up on body fuel. I wanted to make sure to eat a hearty meal, but not so heavy that I'd get sleepy on the road. The hotel actually had a really good spread for a breakfast, definitely a higher end of assortments than most places I've stayed.

As I walked around the buffet table, loading up my plate, I felt out of place. I was all decked out for riding, and everyone else was dressed to impress. Though I've gotten used to the contrast of the classy European style versus my comfortable way of dressing, I still felt a bit self-conscious at times.

After my meal, I took my bag and gear to the bike, strapped it up, and mounted the beast. I had two stops to hit today prior to beginning my journey home. I fully intended to stop for the night at some point. Yesterday was long—maybe too long—and I didn't want to risk my safety just to get home early. First stop, ProBike, a.k.a. the Malmö Harley Davidson dealership.

After a short ride, I arrived at the ProBike shop. First off, the staff were so much nicer than the staff at the dealership in Hamburg. They were very laid back, and I struck up conversations with many of them. They liked the fact that I'd ridden all the way from Belgium, using their location as my final destination. After chatting it up, I did some shopping for souvenirs, and looked for T-shirts for Glo and myself. I tried to find patches or pins, but they had none in stock. One of the staff suggested I ride about three hours north to Gothenburg, Sweden, for some pins and patches. I thanked them, but I had to get back on the road—no detours this time around.

The shop was fairly large, and they sold all manner of bikes and gear, not just Harley merchandise. In fact, the Harley Davidson section was quite small in comparison to the rest of the items for sale. I did look for some rain gear for the ride back, but they didn't have my size, so I'd have to rough it again if it rained on the way home.

MALMÖ–HOME ✯

After about half an hour in the store, I jumped back on the road en route to Cap's Harley-Davidson in Copenhagen. Before crossing the Øresund Bridge, I decided to stop and snap some pictures. I couldn't get a picture of my bike and the bridge because parking was so far away from the shoreline, but I did get a selfie with the bridge and some nice shots of the surrounding area. I had to use my phone camera, having left my Canon behind because I hadn't yet figured out how to get it packed on my bike so that I would have easy access for impromptu stops and breathtaking landscapes. My phone takes pretty good pictures, but I wanted the feel of the Canon in my hands to capture these sights. Using my phone felt cheap, too easy, and unfulfilling for this journey.

I had a lot to do before turning homeward, so I didn't hang around very long—before I knew it, my butt was back in the saddle. I topped off the gas tank right before getting to the bridge, so I was set to hit Cap's H-D store and the road beyond. As I made my way toward the incredible bridge, I already started to feel the soreness envelop my body. How was it that my tailbone was already aching and I'd barely started the day riding?

I rode over the long and windy bridge back to Copenhagen. Traffic was considerably light, considering it was tourist season and I had to ride through the city center. I made my way to Cap's Harley shop and pulled around back where it looked like the employees parked. The store was located in a rundown industrial neighborhood, so I had no issues in taking extra pains to park my bike in the safest-looking area. The shop was very compact; the show floor, chock full of bikes, was butted up against the merchandise display area. This was easily one of the smallest Harley shops I'd seen.

The shop manager was very cool; she and I chatted about my trip for a bit before I purchased a couple of shirts. Like ProBike, Cap's had no patches or pins, but she said I could order them online when they arrived in stock. After making my purchases, I popped a squat on their couch with a coffee and a flipped through a hefty catalogue. This was my last relaxing stop before riding to the Rodby ferry port, which would take me to Puttgarden in Germany.

While relaxing, I saw a bike on the shop floor with the rearview mirrors underneath the handlebars—it looked crazy. *I* could imagine my bike with the inverted mirrors and the GPS moved to the center of the handlebars. I decided then and there to invert my mirrors when I got a chance. After my break and a good stretch, I got back on the road; this time, the destination was home.

MALMÖ–HOME

I left the city of Copenhagen and rode through the countryside with the sun shining bright. As I raced toward the port, I absorbed the warmth of the sun and drank in the beautiful scenery. It was just so invigorating to see all the greenery, water, bridges, and blue skies.

While in Denmark, my thoughts turned to an ex-girlfriend from college; she was born and raised in Denmark. Her hometown wasn't too far from Copenhagen but far enough away to avoid big-city issues. We'd parted company years ago and had both moved on, but the way it ended was so weird that I sometimes found myself thinking about it. She was a sweetheart, and I was pretty immature back then. I was set to graduate and commission, which meant leaving San Antonio, Texas (where the college was that we both attended) for greener pastures.

Even though I really liked her, I acted pretty nonchalant about our relationship. I took her companionship for granted; so, when she unexpectedly broke it off with me, I was shocked and heartbroken. She wanted to remain friends, but when I realized that we weren't going to reconcile, I didn't want her in my life at all. I was hurt and angry, but mostly I was ashamed. I knew that I'd messed up; I knew that I hadn't been my best self for her, and I didn't want to be reminded of it.

Years later, I reached out and reconnected with her. We chatted for quite a while, catching up on her life and mine. She was living a very happy life, and I was truly happy for her. I apologized to her for how I'd behaved in our relationship, and without hesitating, she forgave me. I felt a huge weight lift off my shoulders and a closure to that chapter in my life. Now back in Denmark, I thought about riding through her town on my way to the port, just to tell her that I had visited her hometown. But I had a long road ahead and was already feeling the soreness all over my body. I'd have to reach out to her later and let her know that I rode all over her country on my bike; she'd appreciate that.

The ride to the Rodby ferry port was not too long, and after one stop for gas just before the port area, I pulled up to the ferry entrance to Puttgarden. Being that this was my first time taking a vehicle (of any kind) on a ferry (of any kind), I was feeling a little nervous that it would be a long and difficult process, especially when adding in the language barrier. I hadn't researched the ferry-boarding process ahead of time, so this was all new to me. I quickly realized, though, that I had nothing to worry about. I bought my ticket without any hassle and was directed to jump to the front of the vehicle line because I was on a bike and could split lanes.

While waiting for the next ferry, a group of riders pulled up beside me. They looked like they had either already ridden a long ways or were preparing for a long ride. While we didn't really chat, they seemed like cool people. Once the ferry offloaded the vehicles arriving from Germany, we rode our bikes to the bike spots in the belly of the boat. I watched the other riders strap their bikes down, so I followed their lead. One of them even came over to help me out; I guess he could tell I was new to the ferry system.

My bike rested on the right-hand side of the ferry, and I strapped it down as tight as I could. The last thing I wanted was for it to fall over in transit. After I secured the bike, I went up to the deck to grab a bite to eat. Following the mass of passengers up the stairs, I came out into the main area. There were places to eat to the left and right of the stairs, so I chose to go right. I ended up at a buffet that was available for the duration of the transit.

I paid for my meal, grabbed a table for one with a front-row view of the journey, and proceeded to grab a plate. I was really hungry, so I was slightly disappointed that the food was just "OK"; instead of eating to enjoy the food, I ate to fill up my body's gas tank. I grabbed water for hydration, apple juice for some sugar, and coffee for the caffeine to enjoy with my meal. After I ate,

I kicked back and tried to find a Wi-Fi signal; no such luck. I needed to reach out to Glo because I completely forgot to message her this morning before I left the hotel. She might be worried, but more likely she was just chilling. I did want to reach out sooner than later, though, just in case.

After the 45-minute ride across the Fehmarn Belt strait, I was back on the bike, riding out of the belly of the ferryboat and on the road toward home. The sun still shone high and bright, but I could see some darker clouds far off in the distance ahead—I could only hope I would miss whatever it was, because it looked pretty menacing.

After almost two hours on the road, I needed to fill up again, so I pulled off, gassed up, stretched a bit, and then hit the road again. I cranked up my music and cleared my mind of any thoughts—just letting my mind drift along with the currents of the musical rhythms and feeling the freedom of the open road. As I approached Hamburg, Germany, I began to worry that I would encounter construction and more traffic on the highway. Thankfully, I had no reason to turn off and detour through the city; the highway took me straight past the city with no delays. By the time I'd passed Hamburg, those dark clouds appeared much closer, and it didn't take a lot of experience to know that I was headed for rain pretty soon. I decided to find a place to stop for food and a good stretch before getting uncomfortably soaking wet.

I pulled off the highway at the next large rest stop after passing Hamburg. After fueling up the bike, I hit the restaurant—parking in front—and made my way inside. I decided to get another hearty meal: German schnitzel and potatoes. Once I paid for my food and drink, I found a spot to sit.

I peeled off my gear and plopped down to eat and to contact Glo. To say that Glo was pissed is a gross understatement—she was livid. Apparently, she had been worried the entire day; crying and all. She had made plans to go to the movies with some friends but cancelled because she was so worried that something bad had happened. She called a few of my coworkers and hacked my Facebook account to see if anyone knew where I was or to see if I had messaged anyone about anything that had recently happened. She even told me that if she hadn't heard from me by 2300, she was going to call my job and report me missing. YIKES!

First, calling my workplace would've been really bad. Had she called to report me missing, more than likely the report would have catapulted all the way up to the U.S. Air Force General in charge of all the troops in Europe. So, just imagine having to stand in front of and explain the situation to your boss, your boss's boss, your boss's boss's boss, and finally, the last boss's boss—that would've given me a really bad kink in my already troubled career.

Second, I felt pretty crappy about being the cause of her worry and concern. I'd meant to message her in the morning and just plain forgot. Even when I realized that I hadn't messaged her, I didn't think it was that big of a deal. She never really expressed any huge concern about the trip beforehand, so I just assumed that she wasn't all that worried. Bad assumption on my part—really bad.

When I called, she was initially very quiet and moody. I had no idea what she was upset about; I figured she was just cranky. But after some prying, I got her to open up about her frustration. After listening to her fraught-with-worry explanation, I apologized, and then we hung up. I decided to call her back and apologize again for being so inconsiderate; I really had no idea she'd spent the day stewing in a worrisome broth. She tends to hold onto the hurts and wrongs done to her—intentional or not—and will brood on them for days. I lightened up the conversation, looking to build a bridge out of the doghouse I was in and into the people-house I hoped to reenter.

After some effort to lighten the mood, we chatted for a bit while I ate another Schnitzel. (I was very hungry—don't judge me.) I told her where I was on the road, and because I was already well past Hamburg—and I felt really good—I decided to keep the momentum going all the way home. I said my goodbyes, told her I'd be home soon and not to worry—or call my job—and then I hung up. I finished up my food, hit the bathroom, and geared up. I stretched my back, legs, and glutes with each step toward my bike. With one final big stretch, I hopped on the bike and hit the road.

Back on the road, I began thinking about my relationship with Glo; specifically, our communication. I'd really messed up today. And even though I fully expected her to ham it up, elevate her worry to the nth degree, and milk it for everything it was worth, I really did feel like crap. I've always lived alone before we began dating, so I wasn't used to being accountable to someone else. I'm also a very independent person. Being an only child, I learned long ago not only to be comfortable with my independence but to enjoy it, too.

To be clear, my independence isn't the main problem; it's that I can be quite selfish at times, in the name of independence. We've been together for about six years now, and I still struggle with this unintentional selfishness. Growing up as an only child, I had been trained by my mother early on to be self-sufficient and independent. She didn't want me to have to depend on anyone for anything; that independence came with the freedom of mind and accountability to no one but myself (with the exception of the law, of course). When living my life and doing the things I wanted, I never stopped to consider how my independent actions affected those around me. I lived in a bubble of self-accountability.

To take it a step further, how often do I do things within our relationship that show the same lack of consideration for how she feels? I mean, just because she doesn't voice it doesn't mean she isn't feeling it, right? I had some new insight to consider about myself in the context of my relationships. I think the biggest sin to Glo wasn't that I forgot to message her but that I made an *assumption* regarding how she felt, without considering how SHE felt. I let my lens of "independence" dictate how I thought she *should* feel, which is not very empathetic. Today, I learned quite a bit about myself and was appreciative of my newly gained insight.

That wall of dark clouds I spotted on the horizon earlier were now straight ahead—my hopes and silent pleas to miss the storm completely were denied. There were large patches of rain on the highway—each time I hit a stretch of rain, I slowed down and moved to the far right lane. I wanted to ensure I was out of the way of the motorists who were driving like maniacs in the inclement weather.

MALMÖ–HOME ★

As the rain began to let up and I became more confident with the conditions, I slowly increased my speed until the next patch of intense rain hit. I tried in vain to buy rain gear at the ProBike store, but I completely forgot to look for some at the Harley shop in Copenhagen. All I could do when I left the restaurant was to put the rain cover over the roll bag so at least my stuff would remain dry, even if I wasn't going to be.

During this dreary stretch, I couldn't let my mind drift as I had earlier; I needed laser focus on the road underneath me and the cars and traffic around me, and I also tried to stay as warm as possible. This intense level of concentration required a lot of energy, so I knew riding in this weather was going to leave me doubly exhausted.

About two stops later and approaching the edge of The Netherlands/Belgian border—soaking wet, freezing cold, and exhausted—I pulled into the final gas station about three kilometers from the Belgium border. I'd ridden long and hard in terrible conditions. My body was frozen stiff, so it took some effort to get off the bike and peel off my gloves at the gas pump.

After filling up, I left my bike at the pump and shuffled into the gas station to pay and get some much needed coffee. I wrapped my fingers around the coffee cup, trying so hard to sap the warmth from the piping-hot coffee in the cup through to my naked, cold, and prune-like fingertips. I was so close to home I could feel it; even still, I dreaded getting back on the bike. I was in pain! But, it was time to leave the station and trudge back to my big, bad, and beautiful bike. It sat there at the pump, beckoning me to finish strong. Sore and beaten up, I threw my leg over the seat and cranked up the engine. I did feel a little refreshed and reenergized; I could even begin to feel the joy growing inside, knowing I was so close to home.

The closer I got to the house, the longer it seemed to take. I caught myself rushing it a bit too much on the wet, slick roads. Riding onto a looping highway onramp, I was going much too fast around the curve. My back tire fishtailed as I came out of the curve, and I damn near wet myself—I've never had a scarier moment on the bike. And, I knew immediately I needed to slow it down. Any weariness I had been feeling was gone in an instant, and I was now on high alert, taking it much slower. I quietly thanked God that I hadn't wiped out on that curve and continued toward home. It soon stopped raining, but the roads remained wet and slick all the way to the house.

About 45 minutes after crossing into Belgium, I pulled into my driveway, feeling so relieved and accomplished. This was just a practice run for next week's

"Ride the Alps" trip, and I crushed it! I was Home! I pulled into the garage, shut the engine down, and gingerly dismounted. I considered just leaving everything on the bike and getting it all tomorrow; after all, tomorrow was Sunday, and I had the day off to recuperate. Nope—I decided to grab it all now; one less thing to do tomorrow because I planned to stretch out on the couch all day.

I removed the rain cover, unwrapped the long straps on the roll bag, took it with me, and walked out of the garage, sore tailbone and all. I could hear the garage door closing as I walked toward the front door. As I opened the door, I was instantly greeted by Watson, my shaggy Australian shepherd. She was more excited about me being home than I was, I think. I set my stuff down in the entryway, peeled off my jacket and hoodie, and gave Glo a big hug and kiss, apologizing again for being the source of her worry and consternation. I could tell she was still feeling out of sorts about my jerk-i-ness, but I could also see that she was relieved to have me back home, safe and sound. That aside, I knew I was looking forward to a hot shower and my soft, comfortable bed. It had been a phenomenal trip, and I could barely wait for next week's!

RIDE THE ALPS

Countries to Travel to:

- ★ ~~Belgium~~
- ★ ~~The Netherlands~~
- ★ ~~Germany~~
- ★ ~~Denmark~~
- ★ ~~Sweden~~
- ★ Austria (6 of 10)
- ★ Liechtenstein (7 of 10)
- ★ Switzerland (8 of 10)

Miles/Kilometers Traveled: 1,309 mi/2,106 km

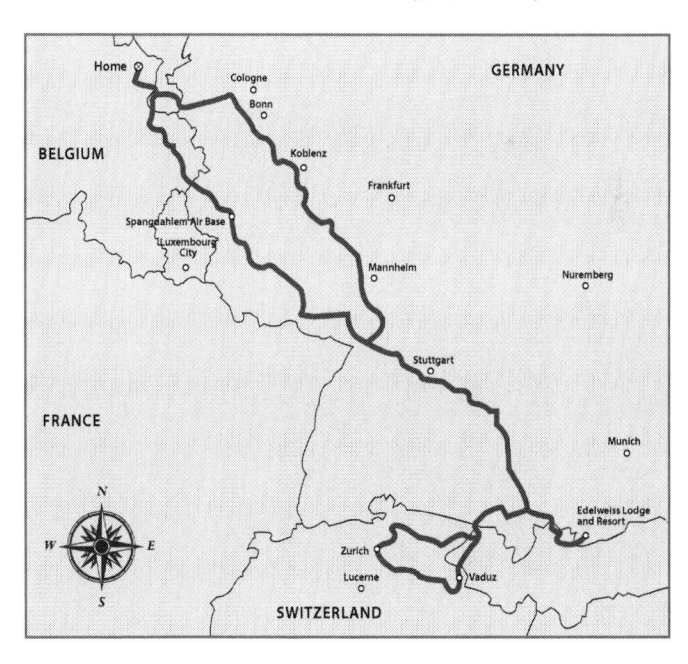

Chapter 4

HOME–SPANGDAHLEM AIR BASE

23 JUNE 2016

Today, my buddy Andy and I are riding to Spangdahlem Air Base in Germany. We're meeting up with two other riders who will ride with us across Germany to the Edelweiss Lodge and Resort in Garmisch-Partenkirchen (Garmisch for short)—where the "Ride the Alps" motorcycle rally takes place. U.S. military folks come from all over Europe to meet and ride in the "Poker Run" on Saturday, play the games, drink beer, and see some amazing sights on the back of their bikes.

I'd been looking forward to this rally for a really long time. I'd missed the ride in 2014 because Glo and I had just arrived from the States, and my bike hadn't shown up yet. I'd missed it again in 2015 due to work commitments, and this time next year Glo and I would be long gone—so this was my last chance to participate.

I hadn't really had an opportunity to look forward to this trip because I'd taken on the project-officer role for my Squadron Commander's Change of Command ceremony. Today is both the ceremony day and the first leg of my trip. I hadn't even packed yet for this weekend, and we were supposed to ride two-and-a-half hours to meet up with our fellow riders after the ceremony. It'd been so busy; this ride was gonna do wonders to relieve my stress.

Because commanders serve as such for only about two years, the current commander's time was up, and we were to get a new one. I volunteered to be the lead for the transition event in an effort to show my continued dedication to the Air Force, even while still reeling from being passed up for promotion. I wanted to let my leadership know that my head was still in the game.

The Change of Command event was a beast and a bear, but also very eye-opening. I made sure that the outgoing commander and his family received a proper goodbye. I even spearheaded the commander's going-away gift—no one else seemed too excited to take the lead, so I decided to run with it—and I have to say it came out better than anyone expected.

For the going-away gift, I had a woodworker carve out a large Belgium-shaped wooden plaque. Then I instructed him to cut it into six fairly even pieces (to be remounted on a wooden backing), to represent each of the five main flights (divisions of the organization) and the administration section. In the middle of the plaque, extended arms were carved out to hold the "traditional" going-away gift that's given. I requested that each of the five flights and the administration send me their logos and something their flights wanted to tell the commander, and then I had each logo/quote engraved on each of the pieces of the plaque. The end result turned out so awesome.

During the commander going-away ceremony (before the actual change of command), each flight individually presented their piece of the Belgium woodwork, said a few words to him, and then put their piece on the larger backing of the wood sculpture that would hold all the pieces. When the last flight made their presentation, the full plaque came together as a Belgium-shaped representation of his command for the unit. Although this commander was a master at hiding his thoughts and emotions behind an impenetrable poker face, it was the first time I'd seen a crack in his facial armor. He was blown away with the gift, and he couldn't hide it. I felt a huge swell of pride that my concept had come together so perfectly. But today was the ceremony for the actual change of command, and it was hectic. Out with the old and in with the new, as they say.

I coordinated quite a bit with the incoming commander, and he seemed very laid back and down to earth; it was going to be interesting to see the leadership differences between the old and the new. That comparison would have to wait, however, because I was hustling to ensure the day went off without a hitch. Once the ceremony finished and all the guests were shuttled to the BBQ at the squadron bar, I made sure that any last-minute details were taken care of, shook hands with the new boss and his wife, and then made ready to head home to pack for my ride. The entire day had been a whirlwind, so as I drove out the front gate headed toward home, I breathed a deep sigh of relief. The ceremony and the party had gone very well, the outgoing commander felt honored, and the inbound boss felt very welcomed. My job was done; now it was time to prep for my fun!

Watson greeted me (of course) at the door, and after a quick doggy rough-housing session, I started to gather my gear for the trip. The trip was just going to be for the weekend, so I knew I wouldn't need a lot of things. Plus, I was riding with a group of people of various experience levels, so I was confident that if I needed anything, someone in my group of fellow riders would likely be able to help me out.

After stuffing my bag with socks, underwear, and shirts, I scrambled around the house looking for any last-minute items that may prove to be useful. I finished packing my bag and loaded it onto my bike. After a last check, I sat down next to Glo on the loveseat in the living room. I thought about updating the music on my GPS SD card, but I was just dead tired from the running around and general stress of coordinating the day's event. I decided that chilling with Glo would be a better use of my time, so we spent some time together until Andy called that he was on his way. He arrived at the house about 15 minutes after his call; I kissed Glo, Watson, and Enwei (Wife, Dog, Cat, respectively) goodbye and took off.

I had never ridden with Andy before, so I was a little nervous because I didn't know his style of riding. He rode an adventure-style bike, so I understood his bike's capabilities, but every rider is different, and I was used to riding alone. He's a very laid-back guy, so I doubted he would prove to be difficult to ride with. We had only a two-and-a-half-hour ride ahead of us—a perfect opportunity to get used to his riding style with little to no stress.

I pumped up my jams in my helmet headphones as we hit the road. Traffic was light, considering it was late afternoon and people would be leaving work soon. After about an hour or so, we made a pit stop at a large Shell rest stop to gas up and stretch. We filled up the bikes and took turns hitting the bathroom so we could watch over each other's bike.

I had been following him on the road up to this point because he had the address to the house where we were headed. After gassing up, he shared the address with me, and I put it in my GPS. I didn't expect to get separated, but I wanted to make sure that if something did happen, I had the ability to find my way to our destination without him.

While we stretched, he asked me what aspects of riding I was comfortable with—things like speed, taking curves, and splitting lanes. I told him that I wasn't comfortable splitting lanes, but that I'd be willing to do it to get accustomed. I thought back to my ride last week where a certain level of comfort splitting lanes would've saved me at least an hour on the road.

After our final checks, we mounted up and jumped back on the highway. Before long, we came to the city of Liege, Belgium. It's a big, beautiful city, filled with churches and historic sites to see. I hadn't taken the time to visit the city, even though I have driven through it many times.

We cruised along toward the middle of the city with no issues before we hit the dreaded rush-hour traffic. I signaled to Andy, who was in front of me, that I was ready to practice splitting lanes. He acknowledged my signal, put on his hazard lights, and pulled into the center of the lanes. With nerves flaring, I followed closely behind him, watching his technique and doing my damnedest to imitate. I did my best to keep my tires directly on the white lines, while my eyes darted from left to right, looking for any cars that appeared as though they may jump in front of us. After a few tensed-up minutes, I began to relax and enjoy the experience. The traffic was actually backed up quite far, but we got through it in 10 minutes flat. Had we been in a car or decided to not split lanes, we would've sat in that traffic for an hour or more.

Clear of the traffic and exiting the city, Andy threw the thumbs up—his way of telling me "good job" for not punking out back there and forcing us to idle in the heat amongst the traffic (it was a very hot day). I used to be really judgmental of those who split lanes; after all, it can be very dangerous. But, it can be just as dangerous sitting in the blazing heat, having all the motorcycle gear on. I understand now why people who don't ride (i.e., vehicle drivers that are simply spooked to have something zing past so close) are adamantly against lane-splitting, but many riders absolutely love it. Not only did splitting lanes save us a lot of time, it became pretty damn fun as well.

After my lane-splitting experience, I gained more confidence in my ability to do so, as well as a newfound respect for the benefits. Besides, in Europe, it's expected that motorists will watch out for bikers splitting lanes in traffic. Seeing the cars nudge to the left or right as we approached from behind reminded me of the scene in *The Ten Commandments* where Moses parts the Red Sea. All you had to do was crank the throttle to let people know you were there, and they moved. Fantastic!

Once we were clear of Liege, the view was stunning. We were climbing in elevation, so we were treated to views of giant hills and mini-mountains lush with green forests; deep, sweeping valleys littered with small and antiquated villages; and snaking rivers and creeks—all against a blue and sun-filled sky. We were enveloped in such serene beauty that I decided to let my mind go blank and just enjoy the flow of my music mix with the beauty around me.

Traffic was light after we departed Liege, and after about an hour of enjoying the ride, we took the exit that headed toward the Spangdahlem Air Base in Germany. We didn't actually go to the base; instead, we looped around the perimeter fence, following the road to a small and quiet neighborhood on the far side of the base. We found our destination—the home of our weekend fellow rider—and parked our bikes in his garage.

HOME–SPANGDAHLEM AIR BASE ★

Our host, Brad, came out to greet us and show off his collection of bikes (two bikes, really; his BMW track bike and his BMW adventure bike).

He used to work at the base Andy and I worked, and we knew him from his time there. He was actually the person who sold Andy his old bike—for an outstanding price, too. Brad was an avid and experienced rider, so I was very nervous about what the ride the following day would be like. He was the de facto leader for the group because of his broad scope of experience, so I was sure he'd have some good lessons to offer.

As Brad was showing us to our rooms, we met his wife, who offered us drinks and conversation about past trips and upcoming travel. Brad threw some burgers on the grill, and the missus made a salad for us to eat. While they prepped dinner, I called Glo to let her know I'd made it safe and sound. I definitely didn't want a repeat of last week's episode, so I made it a point to let her know when I was leaving for the day and when I arrived at my destination, with some extra messages in between. I felt bad because the weather was projected to be complete crap over the weekend in the area we were headed to. But if today's sunny and warm day was any indication, we just might just catch some pretty decent weather. Glo had declined the invitation because she didn't want to be uncomfortable riding in the rain.

While I can't blame her, I would still love for her to join me on one of these longer trips. After our chat, I told her I'd talk to her in the morning before we left, and then went back out to the common area to get my grub on—I was crazy hungry.

After a delicious meal and a movie, we all called it an early night. Retiring to the guest room, I jumped into my pajamas and set all my clothes and gear up for tomorrow. I wanted to be ready to roll in the morning so that no one was waiting on me. We planned to set out nice and early, and we still had one more member of our riding party to meet up with on base in the morning. After all my gear was prepped and ready, I crawled into bed and played on my phone until I felt myself drifting. What started out as an incredibly long and stressful day made me primed and ready to release all that stress on the road in the morning. With my alarm set and my phone charging, I finally let sleep overtake me.

Chapter 5

SPANGDAHLEM AIR BASE– GARMISCH
24 JUNE 2016

Today is the trek to the Edelweiss Resort. I didn't unpack much last night, so it was an easy go getting ready. I took care of the hygiene stuff, got dressed in no time, and then made my way to the kitchen. After morning greetings and a cup of coffee, I messaged Glo to say good morning and to let her know we were about to hit the road. Andy and Brad seemed to be as prepared as I was because in less than an hour from waking up, we were loading up the bikes and setting out toward

★ TWO WHEELS DOWN

Spangdahlem Air Base to get fuel and meet up with the last member of our group, Freeman.

The ride to the base proved to be a preview of Brad's aggressive riding style. I decided right then that no matter what, I wouldn't be forced into anything I wasn't comfortable with. I didn't think there would be any peer pressure, but traveling in a group can make it difficult to accurately judge your own individual capabilities.

Brad was adept at whipping around the tight corners on his bike, getting down low on the roundabouts to cut through. Andy was right there with him, and I brought up the rear; I took the corners at a very comfortable pace. After about 15 minutes of riding in the brisk morning, we pulled up to the gate of the base. It was Friday morning, so there was a decent amount of traffic on base as people headed to their respective work areas to begin their day. We wound our way through the base to the gas station. Andy and I pulled up to the pumps, while Brad pulled off to the parking area where Freeman was patiently—if not excitedly—waiting.

I filled up my tank before heading inside to pay. I picked up a bottle of water and a package of Fisherman's Friend extra-strength throat lozenges. When I got to the register to pay for my fuel and goods, I realized that I'd messed up. I wasn't stationed in Germany, so I wasn't supposed to fuel up because I don't have gas rations for this country—which I knew, suddenly. I told the attendant that I understood if I needed to pay the economy price. He was pretty pissed because I fueled up first and then told him. I was under the impression that if you did not have the ration card, you had to pay the same price as the gas stations off base. (I guess you're not even supposed to do *that*.) But, I caught a break because the attendant couldn't figure out how to back out of the transaction and do what needed to be done to fix the situation. So, the attendant just made a show of force (of his annoyance at me) and gave me the discounted base price, and told me not to do it again. I agreed not to make the same mistake twice. As I grabbed my water and candy, I looked behind me, and there stood Andy, two customers behind. He'd witnessed my exchange with the attendant and realized he had done the exact same thing. We chuckled because we both knew what was coming to him when he got to the counter.

I got back to my bike, loaded the water into my roll bag and my Fisherman's Friend mints into my pocket, and rode to where Brad and Freeman were parked. (I love my eucalyptus Fisherman's Friend lozenges—they're about triple the strength of Altoids breath mints and do a great job of providing a boost and a shock when I start to get a bit drowsy.)

I had met Freeman before, as he was the communications liaison for four different communications organizations. He'd always seemed like a nice guy, but I didn't have much opportunity to interact with him at work, so I didn't know him very well. I was thrilled to see another Harley—he had a Harley Road King. With that beast, there was no way he was going to be hitting the curves hard like Brad and Andy. I figured that Brad and Andy would do their crazy curves, and Freeman and I would just kick back and enjoy the slow roll.

Freeman offered us doughnuts, and we ate, putting a little fuel in our own tanks. Soon, Andy rolled up to the gathering, and he and I had a good laugh about the gas situation—he also got yelled at. Those of us with GPS units inputted the address to the resort; then, after final checks of gear and motorcycles, we were filing out of the parking lot and through the gate of the base to the highway.

The weather was predicted to be pretty wet and cold for riding, but as it turned out, the day was beautiful! We lucked out big time. It didn't take us long to hit the highway from the base and ride it for a bit. Along the way, Brad was determined to show us the curvy and twisty road life. He took us down some side roads that carved through some very beautiful scenery. The German landscape was hilly, but not all of the hills were steep. After about 90 minutes of riding off the beaten path, we stopped for 10 minutes for gas and a stretch—not too long a break before jumping back on the road.

We rode the highway for a while before turning off onto another curve-laden route. This route was heavily wooded, and the curves were much sharper than the previous secondary road. Brad and Andy had a blast zipping through the curves, while Freeman and I took our time with it—neither of us were capable of hitting the curves at the same speeds as they were.

At one point, I thought I was starting to get the hang of taking curves at speed—I began hitting them a little faster, but the feeling of being out of control grew with each curve. These curves were particularly scary because there was very little room for error. We were on a one-lane road, so the oncoming cars were whipping around the blind corners, and I couldn't see them until I was at about the apex of the corner in my own lane. Soon, I was going so fast around the curves that I began to scrape the pavement as I leaned one way, and then scraped the other side taking the curve the other way. Skimming the pavement wasn't the problem, though—I loved scraping the bottom of my footboards. The problem was that I was leaning over so far, scraping and all, that I still veered into the oncoming lane around the blind corners. Terrified and crouched at the edge of panic, I straightened the bike in the oncoming lane, hit the brakes, and then swerved back into my lane. Fortunately, no cars or trucks happened to be coming in the opposite direction at that time; I would've been road kill. My heart was pounding hard in my chest. I slowed my speed down considerably, and Freeman continued to follow at his own pace. After saying a quick prayer of thankfulness, I settled on a speed that fit my comfort level and stuck with it. Brad and Andy were far ahead of us, but I figured they'd slow up enough for us to catch up after they'd had their curve-hugging fun.

Eventually, we caught up to—and passed—them. They had turned off the road to wait for us, and not knowing that they stopped, we blew by them as they waved. But before long, they caught up and jumped back in front. We came out of the wooded hills, into sprawling farmland, and then through a few small towns and villages in order to get back to the highway.

On the way toward the highway, we hit a gas station to fill up. While we topped up, I told the guys my tale of harrowing danger on the curves. I let them know that I'd be taking those kinds of curves much slower from now on, and Freeman agreed that he was comfortable going a little slower, too. Brad and Andy understood;

our bikes just weren't designed for that type of riding, whereas theirs were.

We didn't stick around long at the station; we hopped back on the highway after filling up. We ventured through one more detour of green hills and curvy roads before returning to the highway for the remainder of the ride. On each detour, I pushed the envelope a little more, looking to crack some of the boundaries in my way of unleashing my full rider potential. I wanted to get more comfortable on my bike, and not just on the highway. The off-highway areas Brad led us through were really beautiful, and it gave me a playground to hone my skills and build my confidence—though it was clear that Brad and Andy enjoyed the curves more than I did.

Back on the highway, we came to the town of Stuttgart, Germany. Stuttgart was notorious for horrendous highway construction and traffic. Soon after entering the city limits, we ran straight into some of the worst traffic I've seen in a place not named Los Angeles or Houston. Brad began splitting lanes, slowly. He knew that I was still uncomfortable with lane-splitting, but I'd already told him that I would do it to help increase my comfort level. In truth, the small section of lane-splitting on the highway with Andy the day prior had helped a lot with my nerves. Plus, this traffic was truly disgusting! There was construction all over the highway, and all the vehicles were being funneled into two lanes—during Friday rush hour.

I followed Brad's lead, and we split lanes all the way through the congestion, nonstop. It was so awesome! Had I let my fear take over my actions, I would have sat in that traffic for three hours, maybe more. Instead, we cut right through it all in about 20 minutes! On top of drastically cutting our travel time, I actually began enjoying the act of splitting lanes.

Once we cleared the traffic, I began thinking about my friends Robyn and Michiel, who were going to meet us at the resort. They had put their bikes on a trailer because Robyn rode a sport bike (really uncomfortable for long trips) and Michiel had a restored classic (also not good for long-distance riding). They'd driven up to Ramstein Air Base from Belgium yesterday to get a head start. I wondered if they were already at the resort or if they were stuck somewhere in this mess of twisted construction, heat, and long traffic lines. I kept an eye out for their truck as we weaved in and out of the lanes, but I didn't see them. Before I knew it, we were out of the traffic jam and on the far side of Stuttgart.

Amazingly, the weather held up nicely as we made our way across southern Germany and into Austria. Again, I began to think about Glo sitting at home when she could've been here with me enjoying this crazy ride, with beautiful views and awesome weather.

We crossed into Austria from Germany via a long tunnel. Out the other side, the views became mountainous—my favorite kind of views. We hit more and more curves as we wound our way through the upper Alps mountain range. These weren't the massively huge Alps; those were a little further south. But the mountain vistas we were riding through were still breathtaking. The mountain vegetation was small and shrubby-looking—it looked like facial stubble, as if the mountains hadn't shaved in a day or two.

Gazing at the views against a beautiful blue backdrop, I basked in the experience of the moment. As quickly as we entered Austria, we crossed back into Germany. The GPS showed that we were very close to our destination—and it was a good thing, too, because my tailbone was getting unbearably sore. Some of the pain and soreness were remnants from the prior weekend's ride. I found various ways to alleviate some of the discomfort so I could ride for longer stretches without having to stop, including a lot of wiggling and a lot of rocking my butt side to side. I also found that if I sat up straight and thrust my pelvis up and out, it changed the location of the pressure point of my weight. All these tricks worked well enough to get me from gas station to gas station.

★ TWO WHEELS DOWN

As we rounded a corner off the main highway and close to our destination, we hit a huge traffic jam. But this time we couldn't breeze by, because the jam consisted entirely of—you might have guessed—motorcycles. We edged as close to the front as we could to see what the hell was causing such a ridiculous backup. The closer we got, the more people we saw off their bikes, milling around and chatting with other riders.

So, we found the best spot to stop and park our bikes, too. I hopped off and removed some of my gear. After slinging it all on my bike, I walked up the road a bit to see what was going on. As I neared the head of the line, I could see that there had been an accident. I couldn't tell how bad it was because people were already tending to the injured and cleaning up. But, I gathered through visual evidence and chatting with some of the onlookers that it was indeed a motorcycle accident. It didn't look like it was fatal or anything; maybe just someone taking a curve too loose and running into the rail or something. What a bummer to start the weekend! They were probably really looking forward to this incredible journey. I prayed that this wasn't some kind of bad omen.

I made my way back toward the group, who were all off their bikes and stretching, and relayed the information. It was a good 30 to 45 minutes of waiting before we were able to get moving again but still early enough that we weren't in any rush. We could see people ahead start to get back into their gear and on their bikes. Following their lead, I geared up and stood by my bike until I saw people up front starting their engines. It wasn't long after that that we were back on course. Ten minutes later, we rolled into our destination town, Garmisch, Germany.

Pulling into town, we went straight for the gas station to fill up; it wasn't that any of us were low, but we didn't want to have to do this dance in the morning. It was an unspoken agreement that told me I had reached a new level of rider status; after all, riders with a hive-mind make a good team.

While fueling up, we grabbed our reflective vests. Brad told us that the event organizers were very, very strict about riders having vests during the resort ride—he'd seen people being turned away for not having one or for buying a road worker's reflective vest. You'd think that as long as the vest met the intent, they wouldn't be so picky about what it looked like. But, Brad said the organizers go way overboard about the rule. Luckily, I'd packed my vest, so I was set. Everyone else in our group was set (although one had a road vest on; I won't say who . . .).

We made our way to the venue and rolled into the outdoor parking area. There was a cluster of about six parking spots all together, so we pulled in and walked our bikes backward into their final resting positions for the night. The area where we parked was like an outdoor showroom—people were walking around, chatting and admiring the various bikes. I wanted to take care of business before enjoying the scene, so I grabbed my gear and went straight to the check-in; the rest of the group was moving at their own pace, so I decided not to wait around for them. It took a while, but eventually I got my room key and hiked through all the resort's twists and turns to get to my room and set my gear down. When I say that my room was in the far back corner of the hotel, I mean it was in the *farthest* back corner.

It felt good to set my gear down and relax a bit. It had been a long and exhausting ride, so the bed felt especially inviting. I didn't rest for too long, however, because I still needed to register for the next day's events. After messaging Glo, I went down to register and receive my event swag.

At the check-in, they gave me a patch, a pin, and a map. The map was for the Poker Run event the following day. If you're not familiar with a poker run, here's the skinny: basically, you receive a map and a stamp card. You ride to each station indicated on the map; then the station attendant has you choose a card from a deck. Whatever card you pull, the attendant then puts

SPANGDAHLEM AIR BASE–GARMISCH

a stamp of the pulled card on your stamp card. At the end of the day, the riders turn their cards in, and the best poker "hands" are determined. The winners receive prizes and recognition. I was curious about what prize the winner receives for a winning hand—that part seemed very hush-hush.

I had pretty much decided to not do the Poker Run but to do my own thing (i.e., tour Liechtenstein and Switzerland) so that I could "collect" more countries toward my 10-country travel goal. I know that Brad was a little irritated by my plan to ditch the group for the day, but it's my vacation, too, so I didn't feel bad one bit. I had things to do and goals to crush; am I right?

I perused the merchandise for sale and bought a couple of event shirts for Glo and myself. She may not have come on the trip, but she was at least going to get a shirt. Afterward, I walked around outside to look at the bikes showcased in the parking area. There were some beautiful machines every which way I looked, and all makes of motorcycles, too; Hondas, Kawasakis, and Triumphs were all represented. However, Harley Davidson outshone them all and ruled the day! There were about seven or eight Harley motorcycles to one bike of any other make. But I began to realize that while I loved my bike and was proud to be a Harley owner, I was really beginning to appreciate the other bike brands. So many of the Harleys looked alike—right down to the paint jobs! And it seemed as if the Harleys would repeat every four or five bikes while I walked down the rows. I know this may seem like an exaggeration, but it really isn't—there were so many of the same Harley motorcycles that it took away some of the thrill of looking at all the motorcycles on display.

I bumped into the guys over by where our bikes were parked; they were just about to head in for check-in. I gave them a heads-up on where to go and what to do. I also told them that I'd hold some seats for the lot of us in the dining hall, so they would know where to find me when they finished their administrative stuff. I also tried calling Robyn and Michiel, who were supposed to meet us here—but she wasn't answering her phone. I figured they were either on their way or they were enjoying some alone time.

I sat and enjoyed the people- and event-watching. There were riders from all over and from all walks of life. Even though just about everyone at the event had some form of military affiliation, it was cool to see such a diverse collection of people. After a while, the fellas showed up, and I bought the first round of beers to celebrate the completion of a long ride and the excitement of the upcoming ride the next day. I invited a guy who was sitting alone at a table next to ours to join us, and after a round of introductions, he became a temporary member of our group.

After the event registration closed, the organizers gave the riders a little briefing to familiarize us with the weekend's schedule of events and the Poker Run rules, and to basically get us all pumped up. After the brief came the buffet dinner, for which I was more than ready. One person stayed back at the table so that we wouldn't lose it, and the rest of us went off to get food. The day's ride had put a fierce hunger in my belly, so when it came time to eat, I didn't hesitate. We kicked back, drank beer, and ate the delicious dinner.

The organizers also introduced the live band, which played some of the oldies but goodies while we ate and drank. We talked mostly about the ride, expectations for the weekend, and if anyone had heard from Robyn. Eventually, Robyn and Michiel showed up and joined us for dinner. They had got caught up in the Stuttgart traffic, and because they were trailering their bikes, they were at the mercy of the traffic gods. We hung out at the table while Robyn and Michiel finished their food.

After dinner, we all headed outside for a while to take in the view of the bikes in the dwindling sunlight. While walking among the bikes, I chatted with Michiel for a bit—Robyn had found herself a cool boyfriend. He fit in with our group of friends back in Belgium, more so than Robyn most of the time, which I know drives her insane!

Around 10 PM, I called it a night and made my way to the hotel room to prep for the morning. I got all my gear together and then decided to take everything I didn't need out of my roll bag so that it wasn't as heavy to carry in the morning. The only reason I was taking the bag at all was so that I could store any purchases from my planned stops; otherwise, I'd have left it in the room.

I was so stoked to check two more countries off my list tomorrow. This was going to make hitting the goal of 10 countries on my motorcycle a little *too* easy; the idea prompted me to think about that on the road the next day—maybe I should consider some different options to address the ease of the challenge.

I crawled into bed, I wanted to get an early start so I could get in some good riding in the morning. I was going on my own, so I didn't need to coordinate with anyone in the group, which meant I could leave whenever I wanted. As much as I enjoyed most of the day riding in a group, I was really looking forward to hitting the road on my own. I wasn't going to be accountable to anyone but myself, and I wasn't going to have to consider what the "group" wants, if it's different than what I wanted to do. I'm not very good at sharing my time if my selfish interests are competing with a group's interests. Anyway, I was stoked and ready! Good night!

Chapter 6
MY OWN POKER RUN
25 JUNE 2016

I woke up excited for the ride! I was still sore from last week's and yesterday's rides, but I wasn't going to let that slow me down. As I got up and ready, I couldn't stop smiling. I was really pumped about riding my bike through the Swiss Alps. I've gone on multiple road trips in and around the Alps, but today was the first time I was going to do so on the back of my motorcycle. Of all of the places I'd traveled, the Swiss Alps still ranked in my top three spots to be. There was something just so serene, magical, and majestic about them. You can't but feel so incredibly small amidst the titanic, snowcapped mountains.

Getting ready was easy, considering I just had to change my shirt and underoos, brush my teeth, and grab my gear. I was up and out the door in less than 10 minutes, with a little extra pep in my step. I made my way to breakfast; I knew I would need some good body fuel this morning because I was going to be on the road for quite a while.

The Edelweiss Resort put out a really good breakfast buffet, so I made sure to eat enough. I had a juicy omelet with bacon, spinach, and black olives, with a side of crispy potatoes, more bacon, and buttery toast. And, of course, I had to grab some coffee to wash down the delectable spread.

As I ate, I messaged Glo that I was hitting the road in a bit and then began to fully plot my course. I had preloaded a Harley Davidson dealership in Vaduz, Liechtenstein, as well as in Zurich, Switzerland. That was a pretty straight shot, so I began exploring other potential destinations. I considered even going as far south as Italy to hit the famous Stelvio Pass, nestled in the Italian Alps. Brad talked this pass up quite a bit as being terrifying and beautiful. I was definitely interested, but when I mapped it out from my location, I would have had to change my plans entirely to make it there and back—meaning, no Liechtenstein, and no Zurich. I decided that I valued my original plan more than a trip on a death-defying pass—this time.

After breakfast, I lugged my gear to the bike, which was covered in morning dew. I hadn't thought to bring a towel, but the organizers were ready, even if I wasn't— there were buckets with drying rags provided for the riders to clean their bikes for the ride this morning. I bumped into Freeman—he was cleaning his bike as well, readying it for the Poker Run.

We chatted about the day ahead as we wiped down our bikes. He asked if I still intended to do my own ride, and I told him yes, I did. I shared with him my plan, and he gave a nod of thoughtful approval. After I was done drying the bike, I strapped my roll bag on the luggage rack.

Freeman offered to take some pictures of me on the bike with the surrounding mountains in the background, so I pulled out of my parking spot and lined up on the road facing away from the buildings and the other bikes. He took some really good shots. The sky was blue and the sun was rising, so I had a clean backdrop with which to model. I offered to do the same for him, but he said he would wait for the rest of the group. He figured he'd have to do this all over again anyways, so why pull his bike out now when the group wasn't yet ready to leave. Made sense to me. No one else was up yet, and considering we weren't riding together, I wasn't going to wait around. I'd just have to catch them when we met up after our respective rides. With that, Freeman went back to wiping down his bike, and I strapped on my helmet, set my destination for the Harley shop in Vaduz, and set some tunes to be the soundtrack for my ride through the Alps.

Off I rode, out of the town of Garmisch and onto the road of freedom and discovery with Liechtenstein in my sights! This ride marked the closing of my goal of riding in 10 European countries on my bike. Initially, I thought this was going to be a challenging-but-doable feat. Considering I knocked out half the countries last weekend and I could easily knock off the remaining five countries this weekend, I was feeling that—while cool—this wasn't exactly the challenge I'd expected.

It wasn't long before I was taking the long, sweeping curves (that we'd ridden through on the way to the resort yesterday) back toward the highway. The views were breathtaking. The deeper into the mountains I rode, the more the Alps began to uncover and reveal themselves. I wanted to stop so many times to take pictures, but at the same time, I didn't want to get off the bike. I decided that I should probably focus on getting to my destinations for now and then take pictures on the way back. That would be the best of both worlds—I would get to enjoy the ride while I was fresh and the weather was nice, and on the way back, I could stop for stretching breaks more often and take pictures that captured the scenic beauty. I was again kicking myself for not putting any more thought into how to bring my Canon camera to capture these sights. Instead, I would have to rely on my camera phone, which thankfully was up to the task. Before long, I was in Austria, cutting a path toward Vaduz.

While cruising on the highway, I decided to revisit the subject of my "10 countries" goal. It seemed now a bit of a sham to call it challenging. I like my goals to be challenging, with a decent chance that I could fail. If there was no chance of failure, how could I truly look at my life as a life fulfilled to the limit with adventure and excitement? Guarantees have a way of killing the spice of life. When we are guaranteed something—anything, really—we stop thinking about that thing until it is time to cash in on the guarantee. When you buy a car and pay for the extended warranty, the fact that you have that warranty doesn't really cross your mind in your daily life, until something breaks. And when it does break, you are guaranteed the peace of mind that comes with having that warranty honored. We seek guarantees throughout life—be it love (marriage), standard of living (work and home), or happiness (stuff and things). There is no spice, no thrill, and no excitement with guarantees.

I suppose I could've guaranteed that I would achieve my goal of riding my bike through 10 countries—established two weeks ago—by the end of the weekend. But, there's no thrill to that, so I decided to change it up: instead of riding my motorcycle through 10 countries in Europe, I doubled the target number. Now, my goal would be 20 countries. Therefore, even if I got to 10 countries on this trip, I would still need 10 more to cross off my list. And, it's important to note that the countries that I've checked off so far have been very close in proximity to Belgium. Now, not only am I far from completing my *revised* goal, I would have to work even harder to check off the remaining countries.

With that self-conversation finished, the new commitment was made—and it was both exciting and terrifying. I was excited for the thrill of the chase—I felt like a road-hardened lion, hunting and chasing down my prey; it was enough to make me salivate (just a little). I was terrified because now that I'd revised my goal, I was now responsible for seeing it through; and if I were to fail, I'd have to carry the weight of that failure for the rest of my life. It may seem a bit melodramatic, but it's a true testament of how seriously I take my commitments.

I didn't want that kind of weight, so I had some work to do. But first, I needed to get through this trip.

After about two-and-a-half hours riding across and tunneling through the mountains, I pulled into the capital city of Liechtenstein, Vaduz. Another country down! This was exciting; I visualized my list of countries and imagined striking a red line through Liechtenstein—talk about a satisfying feeling!

Riding around Vaduz brought back some vivid memories of a road trip my buddy Brian and I had taken in my rented Nissan truck to Liechtenstein three years prior. Without getting sidetracked by detailing that trip, I can say that we had a blast in this very cool and chill town, and I learned more about wristwatches here than I ever thought I cared to know. This time 'round, I was focused on finding the Harley Davidson dealership and getting a patch and/or pin and shirt.

To my surprise and disappointment, my GPS did not guide me to a traditional Harley dealership; rather, I found myself in a tiny parking lot of a custom chopper shop. I got off the bike, stretched, and decided to check the place out. I had a feeling I could kiss that patch, pin, and shirt I was hoping for goodbye. Fortunately, I was pleasantly surprised by my unintended find. "Bobbers" was the name, and creating bad-ass choppers was his game. He explained that there was no official Harley

Davidson dealership in Liechtenstein. He did have some Harleys for sale, but nothing new and mostly modified.

He offered me a tour of his shop, and I took him up on his offer. We walked around the gift shop while he talked with me about his work, showing me some bikes he had for sale and on display. Then we headed to his workshop. As we went further inside, he showed me some of his signature and award-winning designs. This wasn't just a custom shop—this guy was a world-renowned bike designer and builder.

After the tour, we headed back to the storefront, and he brought out a binder to show me pictures of the bikes he'd custom-made for people over the years. His excitement of sharing his talents fed off of my bewilderment and curiosity. The more questions I asked, the more examples he eagerly showed me. He showed me pictures of him on red carpets with celebrities; at parties, rubbing shoulders with clients worth millions of dollars.

Finally, he showed me pictures of his masterpiece bike, "Monarch." He'd built this bike for shows, and it had swept up the awards in various competitions. Of course, anything award-winning would be coveted by any elite collector. He hadn't sold the original; it sat in the shop—but he'd built another one for a Belgian client, and wouldn't you know it, the guy didn't live too far from me! He showed me pictures of this guy's home and his collection of expensive cars. This shop owner was a rock star in the custom bike world, and I had the opportunity to chop it up with him (pun intended).

I enjoyed the tour and the conversation, but I had a trip to continue. I bought a "Bobbers" T-shirt (which was a little on the small side), and then made my way back to the bike to pack up my purchase and set the GPS to Zurich. I was running really low on gas, so with the new course set, I rode through Liechtenstein en route to Zurich, stopped for gas on the outskirts, and then back on the road I was.

The sun was out, the sky was ultra-blue, and the road was clear. I decided to just live in the ride, the moment, and the music. This trip is the real reason I was out here. In no time, I was in the heart of the Swiss Alps. With the beastly rock formations springing up all around me, I was in heaven, and my mind was at ease. The ride was so breathtaking that I may—MAY—have shed a tear or two for the "beauty of it all. . . ." (*May* have).

My ride took me around two connected lakes (Obersee Bodensee and Zürichsee), which just put the whole scene together in stunning vistas. There is no way to translate the feeling of joy and elation I felt on this ride; in fact, I can say that I've never quite had that feeling in my life. I felt so free and unencumbered by life and its crazy obstacles. During that stretch of road, I felt as if my spirit soared above, drawing powerfully upon the beautiful experience. I was happy—*truly* happy—despite my troubles: being unexpectedly passed over for my promotion, dealing with my challenging relationship with Glo, and feeling increasingly anxious about what the future held for my life. During the bigness of this moment, though, all of that "life clutter" seemed so small and insignificant. It was as if I were being shown that what I was experiencing was what life always had been, currently is, and will always be about.

As I rode away from the lake and toward the city of Zurich, I came back down from the spiritual high I just experienced. I decided I wanted to keep what I had just experienced with me forever—to immortalize that exceptional experience by encapsulating it in my mind and emblazoning it on my heart.

Not long after, I rode into the city of Zurich. I hadn't been here before, but I was liking the vibe it was sending me. It was a very clean city, with a beautiful river running through it. There was plenty of greenery, both along the river (which was a feature the city designers clearly wanted to highlight) and the centrum area.

Shortly after arriving in Zurich, I pulled up to the Harley shop that was on my to-do list. It was located in the heart of the city—compact and tucked away. I pulled the bike up, parked, and made my way inside. I walked around the shop for a while before meeting an Italian sales rep. She showed me where all the merchandise was located and then left me to my own devices. I found some shirts for Glo and me—her, something fashionable and girly; for myself, a normal Harley shirt with a screen-printed scene on the back with the city and the Zurich H-D lion. I also found a nice patch and a pin for my vest.

After paying for my goodies, the saleswoman gave me a coffee, and we sat on the couches in the lounge area. She shared with me a bit of her life and travels, including her time living and working in Africa. I told her of my own travels, detailing a few adventures across the seven continents. I told her of my time traveling to Antarctica, summiting Mount Kilimanjaro, and trekking the Tongariro Alpine Crossing in New Zealand. We chatted for about 30 minutes before I finished my coffee and stood up to get back on the road; I was at the halfway point of my day of riding. Now that I had conquered Liechtenstein and Switzerland, it was time to head back to the resort and revel in my treasures from the road trip. I said my goodbyes to the saleswoman, made my way back to the bike, loaded up my purchases, set the course in the GPS for Garmisch, and set off.

Navigating my way out of the city was more difficult than entering the city. The traffic was pretty bad, and the number of traffic lights seemed excessive. Finally, I made it to the highway and before long was on the way out of the city. Once I cleared Zurich, I stopped for gas and a bite to eat. As I was filling up, an expensive-looking car pulled up to a pump across from mine, bumping some serious music. I noticed the license plate indicated that the vehicle was from the Czech Republic. I turned back to look at the meter on my pump, so I didn't get a chance to see the occupants get out, but when I turned back, my mouth dropped to the ground. There stood two absolutely stunning women getting ready to fuel up—and what's more, they both were wearing ridiculously revealing shorts. I mean, when they stood straight you could see the bottom half of their backsides in their entirety. I had seen booty shorts before, but this was taking it to a whole different level.

I picked my mouth off the floor and pulled my attention away long enough to see that just about every other man in the area was also fixated on the women, drooling. Every other woman in the area was also fixated—but on their men, and the looks on their faces held a much different, angrier expression. I finished gassing up and tightened the gas cap, and as I pulled my helmet back on to go park at the convenience store, I caught one final glimpse of the gorgeous women in the most severe booty shorts I could've imagined. (I fully accept my male creepiness.) I pulled the bike around to the parking lot and walked into the attached McDonald's. I got my favorite meal (two cheeseburgers, large fries, and a bottle of water), found a seat outside with a clear view of my bike, and proceeded to chow down—I hadn't realized I was so hungry. I wasn't in a rush to get back, so I took my time and enjoyed the food.

When I finished my meal, I tossed the trash, made my way to the bike, and jumped back on the road, full of food and good vibes. It wasn't long before I noticed that the sky was less sunny than it had been, and there were dark clouds forming on the horizon ahead. There was a storm brewing, and all I could do was hope that I could get the closest I could to Garmisch before it came crashing down around me. All of the carefree and light-hearted riding went out the window. I had about three-and-a-half hours (or more) to travel before I was back at the resort, and I was not looking forward to the impending rainstorm.

Yup—just over an hour into the return ride, the rain hit. I was ready this time, unlike my first ride. After my last dripping-wet trip experience, I'd purchased new calf-high boots, waterproof gloves without the annoying inserts, and a combination rain-cover jacket and pants. The boots and gloves were nice, but I wasn't a fan of wearing the rain gear—it amounted to a two-piece garbage bag (the suit I wanted wasn't available in my size, so I had no choice but to buy the cheaper suit). At least it's portable and doesn't take up much space in the roll bag.

I hadn't put on my rain gear or the cover on the roll bag prior to hitting the rain, partially because I figured I'd get one more stop in before the inclement weather (but also because I naively hoped I wouldn't have had to). The rain was pretty light, so I rode about 30 minutes more before stopping.

By the time I stopped for gas, the rain was coming down pretty hard. The gas pumps were completely sheltered, so I had some protection from the rain while I fueled up. When I came back to the bike after paying, the rain had let up a bit; it was no longer pounding, but it was still raining harder than a sprinkle. I donned my rain gear and put the rain cover over my bag. Pretty much just a giant plastic bag, my "rain gear" was very loose and uncomfortable. It was functional, but I was worried about how the bottom of the pant leg was hanging pretty close to the engine—if it made contact while the engine was hot, the pant cuff would melt. A few years ago, I'd sat on my old bike wearing nylon basketball shorts with the engine running. I smelled something burning and looked down to see my shorts melting onto the exposed engine, which was plenty hot. It was a mess, and I didn't want a repeat of that episode.

MY OWN POKER RUN

As I pulled out of the gas station, I made some adjustments so that I was comfortable and could keep my leg from touching the engine. I wasn't pleased at how much my attention and focus were being drawn to that damn pant leg, but for the time being, I couldn't do much about it.

The major highway travel was fairly uneventful—but very uncomfortable. The rain came in patches; sometimes heavy, sometimes not. The long tunnels I rode through were a nice reprieve from the rain and slick roads. But it wasn't until I pulled off the main highway that I had to really start riding. For a while, the rain had let up, and the ride was pretty decent. I recalled the deal I'd made with myself earlier in the day to take pictures on the way back. I hadn't wanted to stop at the outset because I was fresh and excited. Now, I didn't want to stop because I was chilly, wet, and just wanted to get back to my warm room. But there were some incredible views—I just couldn't resist capturing them this time around. The sky was still overcast, but the scenery was well worth the stop.

I pulled off onto a wide gravel shoulder and hit the kickstand. I grabbed my phone and snapped away—the bike in the forefront with a line of mountains as the background. The colors in the photos leaned toward cooler tones (I tend to like pictures with colder color balances anyway), but the stark greens of the vegetation at the base of the mountains made for an intense contrast. The pictures turned out awesome. After getting about three or four photos I really liked, I put the phone away and popped back on the bike.

The rain picked up as I got back on the road; ergo, back to my laser focus. The big sweeping curves and winding roads that I'd ridden through on my way out this morning were now in front of me—this time, I had wet roads with which to contend. I took the curves with a very nervous energy, recalling the incident last weekend in which I fishtailed after going too fast on a curve in the rain.

I took the winding road at a comfortable pace, ensuring I had control of the bike the entire time. My body was rigid, and every muscle was clenched, tightly. Every now and then, I'd look back at the long line of cars behind me and feel somewhat bad; I didn't feel bad enough to go any faster, though. There were many cars in front of me going the same speed I was going anyways, so in my head I used them as justification, like, "See? Traffic in front—I *can't* go any faster!" though I knew the truth.

Eventually, I made it past the big curves and back to straight roads, but after about 15 minutes of riding, I realized that I was still rigid from being so focused. I relaxed my body bit by bit, and as the rain subsided, so did my stress. I stopped one more time to take a couple of photos—this time, pulling into the parking lot of a church. Armed with more photos of the big, beautiful mountains, I jumped back on the bike—and on the home stretch to the resort.

Just before I got to the resort, I stopped to fuel up and buy some celebratory cigarillos. The gas station didn't have a great selection of cigars; go figure. By this time, the rain had completely given up on ruining the remainder of my ride, and the sky began to clear—it remained overcast, but the threat of rain was all but gone.

When I got back to Edelweiss, I pulled the bike into the underground parking garage and parked in a spot near an exit door. I sat on the bike for a minute and said a prayer of thanks for a safe return—I recognize that going it alone presented a very real and dangerous risk of something happening and no one knowing. The call of the road, alone or otherwise, overpowers my fear of any danger involved, but I'm not naive enough to have a feeling of invincibility; that's a younger man's game.

I lugged my stuff up to the hotel and ran into my group on the way to the room. They were already kicking back and drinking beers. I left them to go drop my gear off at the hotel room and then call Glo. I kept the conversation short and sweet (emphasis on the sweet), grabbed the cigarillos, and made my way back to where the group was relaxing.

Before I knew it, I had a beer in hand and dinner on a plate in front of me. We laughed, joked, and exchanged our crazy stories of the day. I found out that Michiel's classic bike had broken down between the first and second stops of the Poker Run. Robyn had to ride her bike back to the resort to retrieve the truck and the trailer, and then drive back to grab him and his bike. Needless to say, they didn't get in much riding, and I could tell they were both pretty bummed about it.

Everyone else had good stories and beautiful pictures to show for their day. None of them claimed to have had the best (or even a decent) poker hand, so they essentially walked away prize-less but fulfilled nonetheless. Because I'd gone solo, there was a special interest about what my ride had been like. As we finished up with dinner, I regaled them with the stories of my day, painting the scenes I encountered and remarking about the people I met. The organizers interrupted with some announcements, including who the winner of the Poker Run was. After the announcements, a live band took the stage, and people took to the dance floor after good food, lots of beer, and a day filled with great riding.

No one in our group was much for dancing, so we grabbed our drinks and made our way outside. We walked around the bikes one more time, but because the weather forecast predicted more rain that night, most of the bikes were tucked away in the parking garage and not on display. I broke out the cigarillos and offered them to anyone interested in partaking in a celebratory smoke—Michiel, Andy, and Freeman took me up on my offer. Given that the cigarillos were tiny and cheap, they were surprisingly decent.

I spoke with Michiel about his plans for his bike; he said that he was going to fix it up, but next year he wanted to ride a better bike. His birthday was coming up soon, and he was going to get his license that allowed him to ride a bigger-engine motorcycle. Belgium restricts riders from riding powerful bikes until they reached a certain age, and Michiel was still under that age. (Robyn found herself a young one!) Given the nine-year age gap between Glo and me, I have zero room to be cracking age jokes about them.

After a while, the conversation began to peter out, much like the life of each cigarillo we smoked, so when mine was extinguished, I transitioned my way out of the conversation. We agreed on a time to meet up in the morning at the breakfast area, I said my goodbyes to Robyn and Michiel (as I probably wouldn't see them before we left) and made my way back to my room.

I took some time to lay out my wet clothes and repack everything that didn't require drying. My rain gear had done a good job of keeping my clothes dry, so I really needed to dry only a few items. I called Glo to chat with her about the day and the ride home the following morning. I told her that up until today the weather had been gorgeous, but then I hit rain on the way back to the hotel. She felt somewhat vindicated for having decided to stay home—up to that point she was feeling a little cheated because the weather was supposed to have been bad the entire time, and it turned out not to be. She told me that she hadn't done much but relax and chill the day away. That was a pretty average day in her life, so I wasn't surprised. I was hoping she would get out and spend time with friends, but no dice. We ended our chat with the customary "Love you" and "Be safe," and with everything ready for the morning, I crawled into the bed, under the covers, and into my cozy dreams. I was exhausted, and sleep couldn't come fast enough. Tomorrow was the homestretch!

Chapter 7
GARMISCH–HOME
26 JUNE 2016

Up and at 'em! Today was the "Homestretch," and as sore as I was, I was ready to hit the road. I'd prepped the night before, so it was a quick turn for me to get my gear all packed and ready to leave. As I did my final check of the room to be sure I'd left nothing behind, I peeked out the window. Though it wasn't currently raining, I could tell that it had rained overnight, and the sky was threatening to let loose again at any time.

I made my way down and around the hallway maze one last time, headed toward the reception counter to check out. It was still early, so most of the riders were still fast asleep, snuggled deep in the warm and comfortable depths of the hotel blankets. I shook off my envy and proceeded to the reception counter; the check-out process took all of about one minute. Then I met up with the fellas for breakfast, all of whom were already sitting and eating when I showed up. For a second, I thought I was running late, but it turned out they were just running early. I set my gear down and grabbed some food—an encore of yesterday's delicious meal: an omelet, bacon, potatoes, and toast with water and coffee.

There was not much in the way of conversation while we ate. It was pretty clear everyone was still shaking off the sleepiness and exhaustion from the last couple of days. I didn't mind the lack of conversation; I was hungrily wolfing down my food and coffee—it was so good!

After breakfast, we headed to the garage to load up our bikes. Because we'd done separate trips yesterday, we had parked in different areas within the garage. I got to my bike and strapped down all my gear, opting to put my rain gear on because the weather looked promising for more rain. When I finished up, I put the rain cover over my roll bag, cranked up the beast, and rode up the ramp to wait for the rest of the group. As I exited, I was greeted by rain; this was going to make for a long ride home. I was, at least, grateful that the ride here and most of yesterday's ride had been clear and beautiful. But now I needed to steel myself for a wet trip home. My timing was impeccable, because as I left the garage, the rest of my group also exited, and I was able to fall in line with them. Everyone had gassed up the evening prior, so rather than stopping, we just pressed ahead.

The ride from Garmisch into Austria was wet, slick, and dark. The fact that it was raining and dark, and that there were motorcycles on the road did not seem to prevent people in other vehicles from driving like jerks. Oncoming traffic whipped around the curves with wet tires on slick roads. My nerves were on edge, and I was hyper-focused on the crappy riding conditions.

Brad was leading the group and was riding too aggressively for my comfort level. He was weaving in and out of the lanes, passing vehicles on curves that you couldn't see around in the rain. I wanted no part of it, so I just stayed back, riding at my own pace and comfort level. The others in the group hung back a bit more also, but they were still a lot braver than I. I did NOT want my tires to slip, and I rode like I meant it. I was actually becoming very nervous—not for myself but for the others; I was getting pissed that Brad was riding so aggressively in these conditions. If someone had gotten hurt trying to keep up with him, I'd have been furious.

As we crossed into Germany, the rain began to fade, and the roads dried up—a most welcome change. I relaxed my clenched muscles and rolled back on the throttle. With the power of my engine, I caught back up with the group in no time, and on we rode. The sky still looked threatening about an hour out of Austria, but I could see clear skies beyond.

We stopped for gas for the first time since leaving Edelweiss—I filled KB up and then stretched out. After refueling, I pulled up to the convenience store and went in for some coffee. I made mention to the others of my rattled nerves while riding through the craziness before the rain had let up, but no one else seemed too concerned. Maybe I was just being overly cautious. I still felt it was reckless, but if I was the only one to feel that, then so be it.

After warming up with some coffee, I went outside to take off my rain gear; as I got to my bike, Andy and everyone else had the same idea, too. The clear skies ahead was a good sign that we wouldn't need rain gear again on this ride. Even though I didn't expect to hit any more rain, I did leave the rain cover on the roll bag—if nothing else, I would know that at least my bag would be protected if we rode into unexpected weather. We mounted up and rolled out.

With my aches and pains attempting to distract me from my relaxing ride, I fell into the groove of my

GARMISCH–HOME ✯

music, clearing my mind of any thoughts or contemplations. After about another two hours on the road, we stopped for fuel and a bite to eat. I could tell that everyone was getting a little road weary because the conversation was pretty light, but still good-spirited. I stood while eating, as my tailbone was killing me. The Air Hawk butt pad I bought was staving off some serious pain and suffering, but I could still feel the effects of the long ride on my backside. I ate and stretched and wiggled, trying to work out the muscles that were tight and tired from the road.

Back on the highway, Brad took the lead again. With increasingly good weather, we were making really good time in the nonexistent traffic. After about an hour, Brad began taking different off-ramps and exits, looking for a good side road with the nice curvy roads that he so enjoyed. Being at the back of the line, I suffered the greatest from this accordion effect. (The accordion effect is when the lead bike speeds up or slows down and the bikes in line follow suit. It's a natural part of riding because the riders behind the leader react in their own time.)

In one "accordion instance," I was trying to play catch-up as the guys were changing lanes from far left to far right. I got stuck beside a car on my right-hand side, and it took a while for me to get by it. It felt as if the driver was actively trying to prevent me from reconnecting with my group. When I finally got around that car, I then had to fight my way around a large semi-truck.

By the time I caught a glimpse of the group, they had already taken an exit, and I missed it. Initially, I began to think of ways that I could catch back up with them. Should I jump off at the next exit and try to circle back? Would they stop and try to call me? I was running through the options in my head, and then it hit me—just go home. Why overcomplicate the situation when I was just going home anyway?

The more I thought about it, the more relieved I became. I did enjoy riding with the group—they're good guys—but I do truly enjoy riding alone. I no longer had other people to consider or riding styles to adjust to. I had no desire to hit the exits in search of winding and curvy roads to ride—that was more their style; I enjoy highway riding. I could go fast, and I find it relaxing. We'd had this riding-preference discussion over dinner on the first night at the resort. Brad and Andy were reminiscing about riding the curvy roads. I piped in that I preferred highway riding—nice and relaxing. Brad scoffed, "That's so boring!" I didn't doubt it would be boring for him. I also opened myself to the possibility that later in life, when I was more experienced, I, too, would prefer the curvy and winding roads over the straight, fast highway—but right now I was unapologetic about my preference for the highway.

Now alone and unafraid, I rolled onward toward home. I felt renewed and rejuvenated—I realized that when I was riding with the group, I didn't experience the same sense of freedom on the road as I do when I ride alone. That was quite the revelation. Riding alone added an element of danger, for obvious reasons, but, while alone, I was free from caring for anyone else. I was able to let my mind roam, without reservation, instead of being mindful of those in my group. No wonder I enjoy riding alone so much!

With my newfound freedom, I pressed ahead. Not long after I split from the group, I saw an exit sign for France/Luxembourg—two more countries that I had yet to hit on my bike and that were needed for my now-increased checklist to complete my goal. Riding through these two would give me 10 countries, exactly half of my *new* goal of 20. The cost would be an additional hour on the road. As I debated whether to change course or not, I remembered that I promised Glo I'd take her on the bike through Luxembourg and France to visit the famous Black Forest in Germany. And, while I never said that I would specifically wait for her to go through those countries together on the bike, I decided to use my promise to her as an excuse for not adding the extra hour to my ride. I told myself it would be more special if we rode through it together the first time. But I knew my reasoning was total B.S.—she likely couldn't have cared less, and my tailbone was sore and getting sorer. So, I passed the exit and continued homeward-bound.

After a final stop for gas and a stretch, I hit the final leg of the trip. I savored that last stop a little more than usual. One, I was so sore! And two, I knew the next stop would be home, and I was getting more excited by the kilometer. While I relished the few moments, I didn't linger too long. I popped two Fisherman's Friend mints in my mouth, climbed onto my bike, strapped my helmet on, and pulled out for the last leg.

I was very close to Belgium when I stopped for the break, and I could see the dark clouds ahead. I didn't bother to put my rain gear on; at this point, I just didn't care. I was so close to home that it didn't matter if I got drenched; as long as my roll bag stayed dry, I was worry-free. As I crossed into Belgium, it began to rain again, not too heavy, but it was more than a sprinkle. I pressed on, watching my speed on the curves and swearing that each kilometer felt like an eternity.

About 45 minutes after crossing the Belgium border, I pulled up to the house, so relieved to be home. I walked the bike backward into the garage, bringing it to rest in its usual spot. Before I turned off the ignition, I cranked the throttle twice—loudly. (I loved the reverberating rumble off of the walls of the enclosed space.) It was a great sound on which to end the trip. I slowly unwrapped my roll bag and pulled it from the luggage rack, the long straps trailing on the floor. While walking out of the garage, I dialed up Brad, Andy, and Robyn to make sure they'd all made it home alright. No one answered, so I left messages. I'd truly feel relieved after hearing back from everyone. I didn't have Freeman's number, but Brad did, so I could ask about his safe return.

I trudged to my front door and as I fumbled with my keys, Glo opened it and greeted me, along with Watson. I got a big hug and a kiss for my safe return home. I returned the love and dropped everything I was carrying in the front entrance. Next, I walked gingerly to the laundry room and proceeded to strip everything off, piling all the clothes on the floor to be washed.

Now in my birthday suit, I streaked across the house on my way to the bathroom. I hit the shower and just stood under the hot water, letting it bounce off my chilled skin. Standing there in the shower, I thought back to the trip I'd just completed and repeated my quick prayer of thanks for yet another safe and strong return. I was so stoked—I crushed it! I nailed two long trips in two straight weekends, and I had no doubt about my ability or my stamina on the road any longer.

With 12 countries left to complete my goal (most of which would require longer rides), I was steeled in my resolve to destroy this new challenge I'd set for myself. For now, though, I was going to enjoy my favorite part of any trip, the homecoming!

THE BIG TRIP

Countries to Travel to:

- ★ ~~Belgium~~
- ★ ~~The Netherlands~~
- ★ ~~Germany~~
- ★ ~~Denmark~~
- ★ ~~Sweden~~
- ★ ~~Austria~~
- ★ ~~Liechtenstein~~
- ★ ~~Switzerland~~
- ★ Poland (9 of 20)
- ★ Czech Republic (10 of 20)
- ★ Slovakia (11 of 20)
- ★ Hungary (12 of 20)
- ★ Slovenia (13 of 20)
- ★ Croatia (14 of 20)
- ★ Italy (15 of 20)
- ★ San Marino (16 of 20)
- ★ France (17 of 20)
- ★ Luxembourg (18 of 20)

Miles/Kilometers Traveled: 2,273 mi/3,658 km

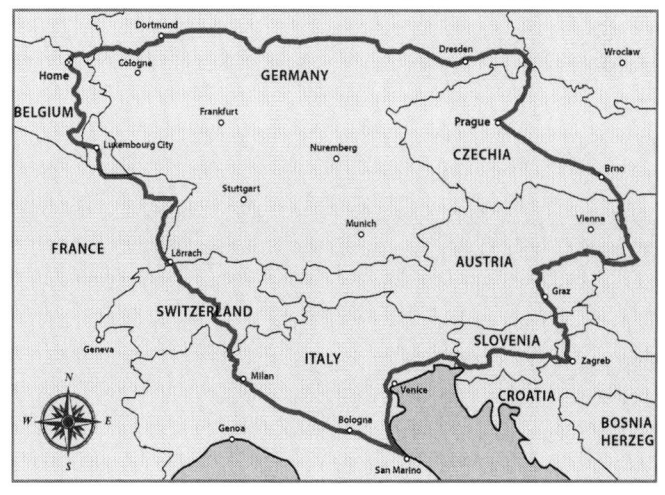

Chapter 8

PREPARATIONS
1 SEPTEMBER 2016

Tomorrow will be a beast of a day! I'll be departing for the longest trip I've taken to date. I'm both crazy excited and terribly anxious. I didn't actually settle on taking this specific trip until a couple of days ago. If I complete this trip, I'll have ridden through 15 different countries in one go, which will leave only two remaining to meet my goal of riding in 20 European countries on the back of my bike. In addition to breaking my personal trip-length record, this trip will also be the hardest I've ever taken. I really have four days to complete a 40-plus hour road trip across the continent and back. It was ambitious, but once I crossed the finish line, I'd be a legend in my own mind!

To make it a little more difficult, I'm doing this trip solo. Glo went to California to be with my mom, helping her recover from knee-replacement surgery. She'd have passed on the trip, anyway; long, rough trips are not her thing. My friend James (who also rides) doesn't have a bike that can handle this type of trip—he's been looking to upgrade his little Honda starter bike for something he can take on road trips once he's comfortable riding longer distances. And finally, Andy had family commitments, keeping him off the road this time around. I didn't mind that I was rolling solo—I actually prefer it, although it does increase the level of risk. But what's a little life without a lot of risk? It also didn't help that I didn't have a solid plan until two days ago.

Since my last few trips, I'd neglected to upgrade any of my gear, but because I had all the essentials, I wasn't too concerned. Anything I needed I could purchase somewhere on the trip. While packing, I had to pack smart with the limited space. I planned to stop at quite a few Harley Davidson shops along the way, so I decided not to pack too many T-shirts; I'd pick some more up during the trip. I did pack plenty of underwear and socks (wool and otherwise); I learned as a kid that underwear and socks were among the most important items to pack, and a couple extra pairs of each never hurt. Since I would be on the road the vast majority of the time, I didn't pack any additional pants—but this time I packed some sleepwear. I learned after the last two trips that not packing some shorts and sandals meant that any time I left my hotel room, I needed to put on my heavy riding jeans and my boots—it was a pain when I needed to leave the room for just a bit. This time around, I made sure to pack some basketball shorts and my flip-flops.

In addition to the normal riding gear (rain gear, extra road maps, spare phone, etc.), I made sure to bring some items for layering. I packed a spare balaclava and left one out to wear on the road. Those were probably some of my favorite pieces of gear—their versatility made them an awesome and valuable tool. I could use it as a scarf, pull it up over my nose and mouth, pull it up over my head as a headband, and so on. And I really liked that the balaclava kept my neck very warm.

With just about everything packed, I threw in a couple of snacks and a bottle of water on top and zipped the bag closed. Because I planned to start the ride straight from work, I went ahead and strapped my bag to the luggage rack on the bike. With my packing complete, I headed back in to make some dinner and relax before calling it a night.

I'd dropped Watson off at the kennel earlier today, so she was all squared away. The kennel we use always seemed to have space for her, no matter how last-minute we called. I didn't like that she would come back filthy unless we requested her to be cleaned (for an extra charge), but now that I know how this kennel "system" works, it's not too bad. The first time we picked Watson up from the kennel, we didn't know we were supposed to request a bath for her—she reeked so bad, I gagged a few times in the car ride home. I was furious! She was clean when we dropped her off, so naturally I expected to get her back in the same condition. Now we have the system down pat—and haven't made that mistake again.

As I was making dinner, I called Glo. California is about nine hours behind Belgium, so she was just getting up to start her day, taking care of my mom after her double knee-replacement surgery. Glo was originally supposed to be there for two weeks; then she opted to extend—once—for another two weeks and now is considering extending her stay again for another three to four weeks. During the course of our conversation, I told her that I took Watson to the kennel in preparation for my upcoming trip and—somewhere out there—a bell rung, and our fight commenced.

Glo was convinced I hadn't told her about my trip. She was pissed and accused me of not keeping her in

PREPARATIONS ✯

the loop of what I was up to while she was away. The problem was, I *did* tell her I was taking a trip, and I remembered doing so. I hadn't told her the specifics, but only because I hadn't fully shaped the trip when we discussed it. She admitted that she thought I meant I was doing a Sunday ride with my Harley Owners Group chapter from the town of Genk. (Every Sunday the HOG chapter gets together for pre-planned rides; they're a blast, and the people are incredibly friendly.) As soon as she spoke the words, I knew it was a simple misunderstanding. I told her as much and apologized for any miscommunication on my part.

Okay; so what should've been an easy fix turned into a full-blown argument. Even though she'd just admitted that a conversation had taken place, she refused to let it go—poking me in the chest over and over again about the crossed communication. There was nothing I said or could say that was good enough; she acted as though I withheld information about my trip because I didn't care about her or our relationship. I tried again and again to explain the problem away—only to fall on deaf ears. She was convinced I was acting like a bachelor and a jerk.

As we were going back and forth on the phone, I grew more frustrated, which gave way to anger. I understood that she wasn't having a good time and that she missed home; and I sympathized with her, truly. I missed her like crazy, but does that mean that I have to stop living until she comes back? Did she really expect me to do absolutely nothing until she came home? It's not as if she'd have gone on this trip with me anyway if she were here; quite the opposite—she'd stay at home and play on her computer. Reason and logic seemed to have left her during this conversation; so, becoming angrier and more fed up, I got off the phone.

I was so tired of dealing with her immaturity and constant "Poor me" mentality; I just wanted to shout, "GROW UP!" I also wanted to shower her with thanks and appreciation for everything she'd been doing for my mom, but we couldn't get past these too-stupid arguments long enough for me to get the damn words out of my mouth! Without her here, I did take full advantage of the alone time to recharge my batteries.

After she left, I fell into a rhythm, which saw the house consistently cleaned, and more eating at home, less eating out. And though we had actually been doing well prior to her leaving for California, I found that I was much more at peace without her here. I love her to death, but she can drive me crazy at times, and my patience for her had greatly diminished over time. I decided to clear our argument from my mind and focus on the task at hand: making food.

PREPARATIONS ☆

I finished making my meal, put on a TV show, and fell onto the couch to eat. The fight crept back to the forefront of my mind. It was a damn misunderstanding; if she couldn't get over it, that's on her, but I refused to let her ruin my down-time. I bust my hump at work, day in and day out, and while I wish I could be in California with my mom, there's just too much to do. The only reason I was going on this trip was because I had a four-day break over the Labor Day weekend. On top of that, I have a shift tomorrow that is on the first down day! *That's* the only reason I'm taking a day of leave on the following Tuesday—so I can get a four-day break for this trip. Feeling the anger begin to rise again, I pushed it back and chose instead to enjoy dinner and some TV.

After my meal, I picked up the kitchen and made sure the living areas were as clean as I'd want them to be when I returned from the ride. I checked that my cat's, Enwei, food and water levels were good ahead of tomorrow, and picked her up as I made my way to the bedroom. I love coming home to a clean house; it actually reduces a lot of stress from the day to come into a clean area. I'd likely be plenty stressed after this next trip, so I wanted it to be really clean. The last item on my to-do list before heading to bed was to update the music on the SD card in my GPS, so I downloaded a couple of new albums that I wanted for the road. After the download was complete, I made my way to bed.

I was starting my 12-hour shift two hours early so that I could be relieved two hours earlier. This meant that I needed to "change over" (take over from the person ending their shift) at 0430. I set my alarm, went through my mental checklist one last time, and then shut my brain down for some sleep.

Chapter 9
HOME–GORLITZ
2 SEPTEMBER 2016

Today is going to be rough. As planned, I was relieved from my 12-hour shift at 1630 (4:30 PM). It was a good start to a trip in which I was looking for things to fall my way as much as possible. As the clock counted down to quitting time, I got nervous that something would happen and the person who was set to replace me would be late, but she was right on time.

After we changed over, I quickly got into my riding gear and bolted for my bike. I was determined to make it as far as I could on the road today. And I wanted to take full advantage of the beautiful weather and sunshine. I jumped on KB and set the destination into the GPS—a hotel in in Gorlitz, Germany, about an eight-to-nine hour ride away. I wasn't sure if I was going to make it, but I was going to give it a strong push.

After setting the destination, I decided to put on the new music I'd downloaded the night before—if I was going to cruise, I wanted my new tunes. To my surprise and disappointment, I couldn't find the new music. I looked for the albums a couple of times and then came to a decision point: do I stop to go back and redownload the music, or do I just press on? I already had to ride by the house to get to the highway; what's a few extra minutes at this point? Back to the house!

I ran in and fired up the laptop. Turns out, the SD card was perfectly fine. The music was on it, but Frank Ocean's "Blonde" couldn't be read for some reason. The only thing I could think of was that the music file from the Apple Store was not readable by the music player in the Garmin GPS. Most of my music comes from Amazon Music, and they use the MP3 file type, while Apple uses an MP4 format. Well, it didn't matter at this point; I couldn't do anything about it, and I was burning daylight troubleshooting the issue. I did my last checks around the house, gave Enwei a final hug, messaged Glo that I was leaving, and mounted up.

HOME–GORLITZ ★

I took only four days of leave, which began on Saturday. Today was Friday, but I was allowed to leave because my duty day was done, as long as I stayed within travel range for emergency recall purposes—I just need to be able to respond within 12 hours if necessary—so I was covered. Friday was essentially a free day, so any ground I could make would be icing on the cake. I mapped the trip as if I didn't have this extra time to spare, so it really was a bonus. Best-case scenario, I'd make it to Zgorzelec, Poland, which was essentially an extension of the German city of Gorlitz.

The hotel I'd planned on staying at was right on the border between Germany and Poland. Worst case, I'd pull into a hotel along the way. I needed to be honest with myself when it was time to stop; after working all day, this was an incredibly risky trip to take. I was probably riding high on nerves, anxiety, and excitement, so I needed to listen to my body when it was stopping time. I mounted KB, ready to conquer a 40-plus-hour ride through 15 countries in four and a half days. I set my music, steeled myself, and pulled out of the driveway in search of yet another two-wheeled adventure.

I made great time on what turned out to be a very direct route. By the time I made it to my first fuel stop, I was feeling good and determined. I wasn't feeling any soreness yet, though I noticed that ever since I'd come back from the Ride the Alps trip, my tailbone was extra sensitive when sitting for long periods of time; I wondered if I had done some permanent damage.

Gassed up and back on the road, I rode like a madman to get the most distance I could from the remaining daylight. Being on a main highway this late in the day, I was able to avoid most rush-hour traffic; any traffic I did hit, I lane-split with ease. With the sun out and very little traffic on the road, I pulled into the far left lane, and let KB roar—I wanted to get to Gorlitz in one go. It was ambitious and (I know) dangerous, but if I could cut out an entire day of riding on my "free" day, I'd be able to take the rest of the trip fairly easily.

While I enjoyed the open road and daylight, I also spent the time thinking about some of the tension between Glo and me. Based on our unresolved conversation the night before, I knew this trip was going to be a huge point of contention for us. She was in California helping my mom recuperate from her double knee surgery. And as I mentioned, she'd extended her stay to continue to provide my mom with quality care.

I made sure to let her know every day how much I appreciated what she was doing for my Mom. I sent her flowers and Belgian chocolates to show my appreciation. But I know Glo; I knew that this spat wasn't really about the miscommunication; it was about her perceiving me as living a bachelor's life without her while she's in the States, slaving away to help *my* mom. Even though she says she understands that I couldn't be there, and even though if she were here she wouldn't have any issues with me taking this trip (nor would she accompany me), it was an issue because she resents my perceived freedom.

I could understand her resenting me for doing things that I enjoy while she's spending her time helping my mom. I would probably feel something similar if I was doing something for her family while she was off having fun. But, I refuse to stop living life just because she might resent me for it. I have an opportunity to put a dent in both of my travel goals, *and* I'm not able to be in California. Just because she's there doesn't mean that life stops happening here. I am a fiercely independent individual—much more than I think she would prefer. And while I acknowledge and appreciate the possible resentment, I refuse to stop looking for opportunities to personally move forward. If she had come back for this weekend, I would've gladly taken her to Greece or Hungary (two countries on her wish list), but because she's not here, I'll use the time for my own travel goals. I fully accept the consequences that may come with taking this trip, because at the end of my life, I want to be able to look back with absolutely no regrets. If I chose to avoid the scorn of my wife, I would've missed out on what could potentially be the greatest adventure of my life. Worth the risk, if you ask me.

After about three hours on the road, the sun hung very low in the sky. As the sky darkened, I let my mind slip back into focusing on the road. I couldn't afford to daydream or contemplate while riding in the dark. Out here on the road, wildlife roamed free, and the last thing I wanted was to hit a deer crossing the highway at dusk.

This thought reminded me of my return ride from the Sturgis motorcycle rally back in 2009. On the way home, dusk began to paint the sky, and the fear of hitting a deer painted my mind. The instructors in the Basic Riders Course stressed that this was the time to be the most cautious about deer running across the highways. They offered grotesque advice for what to do if a run-in with a deer was absolutely unavoidable: "Aim for the middle." I heard stories in which riders hit deer, aiming for the middle, and were able to stay upright on the bike, although covered with blood and guts. I was determined to avoid that type of scene. I couldn't imagine showing up in the hotel lobby in the middle of the night covered from head to toe in blood and gore; not a good look.

With renewed razor-sharp focus, I scanned the road and rolled back on the throttle. After the sun fell completely below the horizon, I rode on for about another hour longer before stopping to warm up a bit and have dinner. The timing was perfect because I was really starting to feel my tailbone getting sore, even with my trusty butt pad. I couldn't begin to imagine what these trips would be like without the seat pad; it makes such a big difference on the road.

While I ate, I stood up the entire time and moved and stretched. I'm sure I looked silly stretch-dancing to no music—but who cares, it felt so good! I also took some time to message Glo to let her know that I was still safe on the road, but I didn't wait for a response—I put away my phone, took a final bite of food, and grabbed my gear. It was time to get going again.

After filling my belly and gas tank, I jumped back on the road. I still had some distance to cover. There was very little traffic on the road this late at night, so I was able to roll on the German Autobahn as fast as I wanted to. All that restrained my speed was the fear of wildlife jumping out of the blackness. I rode the next two hours to the next rest stop so focused that, when I stopped, the exhaustion hit me pretty hard. I had been so tensed up, releasing that tension left me really feeling the negative effects. Luckily for me, this last stop was only about 45 minutes away from my destination.

Well within striking range, I decided to finish out the ride. After some stretching and gas, I popped three

Fisherman's Friend mints, which lit my mouth and throat on fire, and hit the road for the last leg of the night. My focus was as razor sharp as it had been before my last stop, significantly aided by the mints burning away the lining in my mouth. (I imagined these mints as being the equivalent of a shot of adrenaline direct to the heart.) I left my mind blank and just let the music flow, while I put all my energies into scanning the road ahead.

I finally rolled into town late, around 0245-ish. The town seemed like it had a split personality—I rode through some really beautiful areas and then some very shady-looking areas. There weren't many people out and about on the streets at that time of night, so the lack of traffic and pedestrians made getting to the hotel very easy. I arrived at the hotel, which straddled the German/Polish border.

I didn't see any hotel parking other than on the street, so I parked my bike in an area behind a drop-arm gate meant for employees. I might be exhausted, but I'm not crazy—I wasn't planning on risking my bike out in the open in the middle of the night in an unknown town close to a border.

I unhooked/unwrapped my bag and lugged it to the reception desk after locking my bike down. I made sure the receptionist knew where my bike was; I didn't want it towed. She assured me that it would be fine, and she pointed to it on the security screen. With peace of mind about my bike, I finished checking in and trudged to my room.

As I peeled off my layers, I was so grateful that I'd made it all the way to the first checkpoint. I definitely took a huge risk riding after a long day at work, but now that I'd made it, the payout for that gamble was huge: I essentially got a full day's ride in before my trip even started. I messaged Glo that I'd made it and then fell into bed, completely exhausted. My first planned stop the next day was only two hours away, and it didn't open until about 0900, so I didn't bother to set an alarm. I was going to have the longest ride of my trip tomorrow. So, tonight I was going to enjoy my rest.

Chapter 10
GORLITZ–ZAGREB
3 SEPTEMBER 2016

I woke up today feeling well rested, though I expected to feel incredibly sore. Yesterday had been a very long day—a full day of work and then the extensive afternoon/night on the road. Today was set to be an even longer stretch but a much more eventful ride. My plan was to ride from Gorlitz all the way down to Zagreb, Croatia, filled with plenty of twists, turns, and incredible views.

I had some time before I needed to get up so I stayed in bed, swaddled in a cocoon of warmth and blankets. I ran through the day's plan in my head, going over each phase. Today, I'd ride through a small piece of Poland on my way to Prague for a Harley Owners Group (HOG) motorcycle rally, "Prague Harley Days." It looked really cool online, so I was pumped to ride down and check it out. It'd take about two hours to make it there, and the venue wouldn't open until 0900, hence the lack of urgency to get moving.

After the Prague rally, I planned to head down through Slovakia to Budapest, the Hungarian capital. If I timed the ride well, I'd have time to stop at the Budapest Harley Shop for more Harley swag before taking the highway straight to Zagreb, the Croatian capital city. And, if all went according to plan, I would ride through five different countries, all of which were part of my new travel goal of hitting 20 countries on the back of my bike. The primary goals of the day were to get to each country on my list, make it to the motorcycle rally, and get to Zagreb in time for my fantasy football draft (yup—if I planned to pull a repeat as champion in my league, I needed to squeeze in the fantasy draft as a priority amidst the amazing journey I was on).

Finally, I decided it was time to start my day. I rolled out of bed, showered, geared up, and checked out. After checking out, I sat down for a light and, being honest, disappointing breakfast. It wasn't that the food was bad or anything, but the options available just weren't very hardy to sustain me on the road.

I was done eating and on the bike by 0800, feeling well rested and decently fed. I had to maneuver around the drop-arm gate because I didn't have a scanner badge to lift the arm, but with plenty of space on the side, it wasn't difficult.

I decided to top off the gas tank while I was still in the city, and it didn't take long to locate a station. After a very short pump, I set my GPS for Prague via Lagow, Poland. I knew I was on the border to Poland; however, I wanted to ride around Poland for a bit, and the town of Lagow was on the way. I crossed the border, while still in Gorlitz, into Zgorzelec, Poland.

It took all of two minutes to cross the border after leaving the gas station, but the scenery changed pretty quickly. The buildings looked a little older, and the town much more run down. The roads were a little less well kept, and the trash on the streets was a little more prevalent. I didn't really focus on this abrupt change; I'd seen it many times before—traveling from one country to another, it becomes immediately clear as to where the economic priorities lie (or didn't lie). Some of the oldest cities with storied histories had some of the most lax sanitation requirements. There's absolutely no judgment on my part; I understand that for some areas sanitation is a luxury, not a necessity.

About 10 minutes after crossing the border, I found my way to a small one-lane county road that would lead down through the town of Lagow en route to the Czech Republic. The small county road took me through the beautifully lush countryside of Poland. It was still fairly early on Saturday morning, so the weather was cool and the traffic very light. Most of the ride down Poland was on the same single-lane county road used by cars, trucks, and tractors. It was a very relaxed ride, and I enjoyed riding on the gentle rolling hills and seeing the scattered farms along the way.

About 45 minutes into the ride, I crossed the Czech Republic border. Considering the proximity of the borders, the Czech countryside was very similar to the Polish landscape in my rearview mirror. Eventually, I turned onto a major highway that would take me all the way to Prague.

As I started down the highway, I began to see the landscape transition from clean and green farm country among rolling hills to the more populated areas with cheaply made homes and cars, and strewn trash. The closer I got to the big city, the denser the population became, and the more trash I could see. It was a little disheartening to see the trees, farms, and

GORLITZ–ZAGREB

greenery disappear, to be replaced with discarded car parts lying about and plastic bags blowing around the streets. It's the consequence of both a large population (those who couldn't afford to live in nicer areas) and a lack of emphasis/funding for sanitation; seeing it made my heart sink. I knew we had areas like this in the States, where the disenfranchised were forced to live. In America, priorities are placed on making more money for individuals over lifting up our communities—and for that, many people suffer.

Shaking off the depressing spiral, I rejoiced that I was much closer to the Harley rally! I've been to my fair share of rallies (some bigger than others), but I was really excited about this one. Due to my planned schedule on the road, I wouldn't be able to stay for long, but I wanted to see what a Harley rally in Prague looked like.

I pulled into Prague city proper, full of excitement. Unfortunately, the address I had set in my GPS was wrong, so it took me to a very different place than where I was looking to go. I didn't have Internet, so I'd have to find the rally the old-fashioned way: by asking someone.

Since I was already lost, I decided to gas up and ask for directions to the HOG rally. After fueling, I went into the station to pay and was shocked when my card was declined. A chill ran down my back. I was in the middle of the Czech Republic on my motorcycle with a debit card that didn't work.

After my initial panic, I handed the gas station clerk my back-up credit card. When the clerk handed me the pen to sign for the purchase, I exhaled a great sigh of relief. This debit-card issue was a problem, but it would take time to figure out what was up with it. I signed the receipt and asked for directions to the rally. Unfortunately, the clerk spoke as much English as I spoke Czech, so after a couple of failed attempts to convey my question, I waved thanks and left.

Not knowing what was going on with my bank account gave me a tight and queasy feeling in my gut. For all I know, my bank could've frozen my card due to suspicious activity, as they had done in the past for security reasons. What I hoped was that I was simply running low on funds from that account and just needed to move some money over from another account. Standing around thinking about it wasn't going to solve anything, however, so I hopped on the bike and hit the highway toward downtown Prague in search of this "prolific" rally.

While riding the highway, I came across a group of three motorcyclists headed in the direction of the city's center. One of the riders' bikes was a cruiser, while the other two were café racers. I decided to assume that they were headed to the same spot I was, so I tagged along. When they pulled off the highway into a gas station, I did, too, and debated waiting on them or carrying on to find my own way. I had just fueled up, so I decided to strike out on my own again.

I left the station, winding my way through random streets of the city. Many of the areas I came across were familiar from a trip that had brought Glo and me to this beautiful city. That was an excellent trip, with some very fond memories of traveling with Glo. One of the coolest parts of the trip was the beer spa we booked. Imagine the amenities at a normal spa; then add beer—a lot of it. We had a large private room, complete with a hot tub filled with hops, barley, and other beer ingredients, a sauna, a cold shower, and a bed of foliage (it looked like a lot of dried hay stuffed under a bed sheet). But, the best part of the experience had to be the beer taps in the room, supplying unlimited mugs of beer to wash down the delicious beer bread and the relaxation.

Turning my focus back to the trip at hand, I decided to test my Garmin action camera mounted on the bike. I wasn't very familiar with it yet, so I wanted to try it out and play with the GPS remote control feature. I had decided to get an action camera so that I could record some of these amazing trips I was taking. My dad had visited me a couple of weeks prior, and he decided to gift me the money for the camera. It was really nice of him, considering these things aren't cheap. As I rode down some of the main streets, I flipped it on; unsure if it was working or not, I just let it record until I was satisfied with the video I had hoped it captured.

After about 20 minutes of wandering, I found myself at a stop sign, face to face with another biker. I waved him down and asked him about the location of the rally. He pointed me in the right direction and, before long, I heard the rumble of a lot of bikes. I'd finally made it to the rally! Excited, I pulled around toward the massive parking lot filled with parked bikes and large groups of bikers meeting to head out for city rides. As I rode into the lot, I had to avoid a cavalcade of bikes exiting at the same time. I got a couple of dirty looks, but I paid them no mind—I was at the Prague Harley Days rally!

I wasn't very comfortable with the parking situation. There was a lot of foot traffic from the public and a bus stop right in front of the lot. This rally was definitely in the heart of the city. I parked the bike close to the street, definitely not the safest-looking place to park. I guess I had no choice but to hope no one would mess with my bike.

I took my bag off of the bike, grabbed my GPS, locked the front forks, and made my way to the entrance. With my hands full of helmet and roll bag,

GORLITZ–ZAGREB

I paid—heftily, I might add—for my admission ticket and headed inside the rally. I could only afford to be here for two hours because I had a long way to go, and this was only the first stop. *And* the fantasy football draft was like a countdown clock hanging over my head.

I walked through the entrance and was immediately greeted by a pretty young woman wearing the exact same booty shorts as the women at the gas station from my Zurich trip. She handed me a program with a smile and pointed me toward the rally. I have to say, the organizers made sure the women working this rally were incredible looking—most of them could've been models, and I'd be none the wiser. And the one thing they all had in common were those crazy booty shorts! I had to wonder if this was a Czech-specific thing, because I don't remember seeing so many women wearing these shorts in one place. There was no question as to whom this rally catered, and I'd be lying if I said I minded. Luckily, I had all my gear on, so no one could tell exactly how happy I was to be here.

It was still pretty early, so the crowd was still forming. I decided to hit the shops first, looking for a T-shirt, pin, and patch. All of the retail vendors were put in one section, which formed a sort of market avenue. As you walked down this "avenue," you could find everything you were looking for to the left and right.

I found a couple of places and got some rally souvenirs for both Glo and myself. There weren't a lot of vendors, so the market area was pretty small. But the vendors who were there came ready to sell, as their stalls were jam-packed with products. Aside from clothing and knickknacks, there were automotive vendors selling parts and products for the bikes. I perused this section especially thoroughly—not that I planned to buy anything, but I was looking for ideas for my bike. I wanted to personalize KB, but I was struggling because I wasn't sure what I wanted or how I wanted to do it. As KB's paint scheme was unique to my bike, I had no designs to change the color, but I still wanted to customize it as much as I could.

While in the Harley shop in Denmark, I'd seen that bike with the mirrors inverted on the handle bar. I wanted to do that with mine, but the bars I currently have aren't tall enough for the mirrors I purchased. So, I was going to have to find some new bars that were tall enough for the hanging mirrors but still provided a comfortable ride.

After looking around for a while, I didn't really see any designs that sparked any creative ideas for KB. Since it was a little after 1100, I decided to grab an early lunch before heading out. I walked out of the vendors' market and spied a Hooters among a host of other food tents.

I put my gear down on a table in front of the Hooters booth and began eyeing the menu as I took off my heavy jacket. I hadn't been to a Hooters in ages—I think the last time was when I was in high school in San Antonio and the prospect of hot, busty waitresses writing "Breast wishes" on my menu was about the best thing I could ever have imagined. So, it came as no surprise that the food servers behind the counter were gorgeous (much more enticing than the guy at the Polish sausage stand).

I placed my ordered for honey BBQ wings and fries and went back to sit by my gear. While I waited, a French rider, Jean Claude, approached me to chat. He was a rider and a photographer, taking official pictures of the event. So, he asked me if he could grab a couple pictures of me for the rally website. He said I was the first American he'd come across at the rally, and he seemed really excited about it. We exchanged stories of our rides to the rally—he told me that he'd come up with a few other riders, and I told him of the adventure that I was on.

When my food came up, he sat with me while I ate, and we continued our chat. He asked if I would be around for the big concert tonight (some famous European metal band), but I told him I planned to be in Zagreb by the end of the night. He laughed, a little incredulously, and he continued to discuss the concert. As I finished up my meal, we exchanged contact information and said our goodbyes. I made a mental note to follow up and see if my pictures had made it onto the website.

Before grabbing my gear to leave, I jumped on the free Wi-Fi and checked my banking information—I had almost forgotten to do so, even though I'd used my credit card to pay for the souvenirs and the food. Turns out my card was declined because I was running low on funds in my checking account—the best-case scenario. After a deep sigh of relief, I moved funds from another account and double-checked that everything transferred properly. I was so happy that my card hadn't been frozen due to some suspicious activity. Now I was ready to hit the road.

After hiking to the bathroom in the big, hangar-like convention center, I walked through the small Harley museum they had set up. It was pretty slick. There were displays detailing the Harley history, and models of bikes old and new, illustrating the evolution of the brand. After a lap around the museum, I made the trek back to my bike. I wish I could've stayed longer and maybe gone on a ride around the city, but it was time to roll on.

Back at my bike, I gave it a once-over, making sure no one had tampered with KB, and hooked my bag up to the luggage rack. As I was placing my GPS back on its cradle, a mother and her young son walked up to my bike. The little boy, admiring KB, smiled from ear to ear. With his mom's permission, I picked him up and set him on the bike so she could get a couple of pictures. Afterward, I hoisted the kid back to the ground, and somehow his grin grew even wider. I'd just sold this kid's future self a motorcycle, and he didn't even know it. (Mom probably did.) I started the bike, and KB roared to life. The little boy jumped in excitement. As I put my helmet on and waved goodbye, they stepped back. Fully geared up and on parade for this mother and child, I pulled out, away from the rally toward my next destination: Bratislava, Slovakia.

On my way out of the city, I tried to use the Garmin camera again, but I wasn't sure I was capturing anything. I could see Prague Castle off in the distance as I wound my way back to the highway. I needed to practice operating the camera without having to look at it—the last thing I wanted was to be distracted on the road, fumbling with the controls. The real shots I wanted were of the Alps on the way back home and the Italian coastline of the Adriatic Sea. If I could capture those areas on the camera, I'd be the happiest. If I'd had more time, I'd have liked to have swung by Vienna, Austria, to capture some of that beautiful city on the camera. The city was a little more than three hours south of Prague, in the direction I was already headed, but, being on a schedule, I stayed the course to Slovakia. Soon, I was back on the highway en route to the next stop.

Bratislava was a straight shot south of Prague. Before I got to the Slovakian border, I passed through the town of Brno. I'd always wanted to come to this town, as I'd heard that it's a hidden travel gem. Looking at the time, I started to become nervous about getting to Zagreb on time. I was already running behind by about an hour, and adding in the periodic stops, I'd be cutting it close to make it in time for the fantasy football draft.

Once I crossed the border, I had to start looking for vehicle road passes. In short, vehicle passes are a form of road tax used by certain countries. I learned from a previous trip through Austria that these vehicle passes were a big deal, and if caught leaving the country without one, I'd either have to pay a hefty fine—or worse—watch my bike get impounded. That was not an option, so I found a spot and stopped. It took a while, but finally I was able get a pass. They were meant for the windshields, but I didn't really want to stick it on, so I just put it in my pocket. If I got stopped, I could just pull it out.

Because I had to stop for the pass, I decided to gas up. I didn't stick around long, and immediately after

GORLITZ-ZAGREB

getting my fuel, I was back on the highway. I blew through Slovakia pretty quickly, passing by Bratislava without encountering any traffic. I had been to Bratislava on our previous trip to Prague; it's actually a pretty nice city. Glo and I had taken, a train to the city and spent the day exploring the sights. We even took a cab out to the ruins of Devin Castle in one of the boroughs of the capital city. But today I was just riding by, and so with a look at the city from the highway, I turned my attention back to the road and rolled back on the throttle.

I spent most of the ride through Slovakia, letting my mind wander and roam. The weather was nice and bright, so I had few worries. Before long, I came up to the Hungarian border, so I jumped off the highway to grab another vehicle pass—I was pleasantly surprised when I was told that here, motorcycles didn't require one.

Back on the highway, I started to contemplate my time. My intention was to go to the Harley Davidson in Budapest, but now I was starting to have doubts that I'd make it to my final stop (Zagreb) on time. Going to Budapest would cost some much needed time, so I weighed the importance of going to the Harley Davidson shop versus making it to Zagreb in time for the fantasy football draft. I couldn't have both, so at the town of Gyor, I deviated and turned toward Austria—the quicker route. Had I never been to Budapest, I'd

159

have continued on, no question. But I had been there before, so I was comfortable sacrificing Hungarian H-D swag for the chance to draft a championship team.

Drafting a contender team was the biggest draw to make it on time; however, it was not the only one. Another reason I was so keen on getting to Zagreb in time for the draft was that I was the commissioner for the league. This means that anytime there was an issue or problem, I was the one who stepped in to solve problems and make decisions. The draft is a very sensitive time—issues had come up in the past that required a quick resolution. If something happened during the draft and I wasn't available to resolve it, I'd have nine grown kids at my throat when I got back to civilization. With the large time zone difference, I have woken up to 100-plus messages from my league bickering back and forth, waiting for me to dish out directions. I say all this because I actually love my league, and the people in it are a blast to play with, year in and year out. But, getting to the draft on time could save me a lot of griping and backtracking later.

Gyor was only about 30 minutes or so from the Austrian border, so I was close. After another easy border crossing, I gassed up and got another pass for the bike. I also tucked this one into my pocket; I didn't want to cover up my windshield. Armed with the pass and a full tank of gas, I got back on the road.

GORLITZ–ZAGREB

The weather was amazing! The sun was out in full effect, accompanied by bright blue skies. I was in a fantastic mood and could feel the warmth of the sun on my face, even through the helmet. The blue skies were dotted with clouds that seemed to take on many familiar shapes. I'm pretty sure I spotted at least five different bunnies among the countless shapeless blobs.

As happy and relaxed as I was on the bike, I also felt slightly panicked. I knew now that I'd made the right choice to divert my course, but even still, I was going to cut it uncomfortably close to draft time. It almost seemed a bit silly to be worrying about making a fantasy draft while riding around the rolling hills of the Austrian countryside with the sun shining bright. But understand that, on the road, your thoughts will wander and ping on even the most inconsequential of thoughts. I decided to clear my mind of all clutter and just ride with the current of my music, the road, and the beautiful weather.

I cut a swath through Austria by way of Graz and into Slovenia, through the city of Maribor. As I crossed into Slovenia, I began to celebrate and cheer in my helmet—I was so ecstatic to be here! Why, you ask? Slovenia was the only country on this trip I hadn't already visited, in any capacity, so I was doubly excited to hit it. I was making progress on my two travel goals simultaneously, and crossing the Slovenian border meant striking another country from one list (travel challenge with my coworker Bobby) and adding it to another (twenty countries on the back of KB).

Slovenia was surprisingly stunning. I hadn't heard anything about the country and hadn't done much research, so I had no idea what to expect. The rolling hills were lush with thick green forests, and it was beautiful. I was awestruck at the beauty of this country, doubly so because I was on the back of my bike.

As I admired the scenery surrounding me, I felt a renewed sense of delight and my energy levels being replenished. I rolled back on the throttle with a new sense of wonderment. What little research I had done on the sights of Slovenia revealed the beautiful city of Bled and its castle on the lake. The pictures I saw were quite impressive, and I was determined to see it in person, but I just didn't have the time on this trip. It was a bit of a bummer, but I was resolved to come back to Slovenia, and would make sure to spend ample time around that town, its lake, and the castle.

With the sun beginning its descent in the sky and the time until my draft ticking down, I carved down through scenic Slovenia and crossed over into Croatia. Earlier this year, Glo and I had flown into Zadar and road-tripped up and down the Adriatic Sea coastline as far south as Montenegro, passing through Bosnia and Herzegovina. Along the way, we stopped at the Plitvice Lakes National Park, Split, Dubrovnik, and Herceg Novi. We managed to visit quite a few of the *Game of Thrones* filming locations, a television series we both really enjoy. During that entire trip, I don't remember seeing one speed camera or highway cop. So, armed with my experience on Croatian roads, I reveled in my freedom to speed.

As I zipped away from the border toward the capital, Zagreb, the sun seemed to be doing some speeding of its own. Now, time wasn't the only opponent I was racing against—the sunset decided to join in. I really didn't want to be on these roads at night; I was unfamiliar with the area and the wildlife. I can't imagine it'd be too different from Germany, but I was only speculating.

I rolled into Zagreb as the sun had almost completely set. Unfortunately, I was too late to hit Zagreb's Harley shop for a shirt and a pin, and because they were closed the following day, I knew I'd completely missed out. I pulled into the hotel parking lot about five minutes before the draft was supposed to start.

Hurrying, I unstrapped my bag from the luggage rack, locked down my bike, and raced into the lobby. There was no one in line, so I went straight up to the reception counter. The clerk seemed to be moving incredibly slow; tapping my foot rapidly was all I could do not to scream, "Oh, my God—will you hurry up!" Before the room key hit my hand, I was already saying my thank yous and goodbyes, my body twisting toward the elevators. By the manner I power-walked down the hallway to my door, you'd have never believed I just spent the entire day on my motorcycle. I burst through the door, dropped my roll bag and helmet on the bed, and logged into the hotel Wi-Fi. Once I connected, I logged into the draft site, praying I'd make it in time for my first pick and avoid any technical issues. Before I knew it, I saw the "logged in" symbol, I was in!

The draft had already started and was in the sixth round. But, because I'd traded away all of my early draft picks last season to win it all, this was the round in which I'd be drafting my first player anyway, and I logged in two draft picks away from my first pick. Whew—talk about "At the buzzer!" I couldn't believe that I'd actually made it in time!

Relaxing after my first selection, I ordered pizza and a beer, stripped myself of my riding gear, and kicked back for the rest of the draft. After completing what felt like a strong draft, I bid my league goodnight. Then I called Glo and chatted with her for a bit while I finished off my meal. The tension with her was still as thick as ever—no signs of subsiding any time soon.

GORLITZ–ZAGREB ✯

After we said goodnight, I laid back and soaked in the day. It felt amazing to have covered so much ground in a day. I mean, at this time yesterday, I'd been on my way to Germany. I'd ridden through gorgeous scenery, feeling the amazing weather, attended a huge Harley rally, and to top it off, I'd been able to beat the clock and make my fantasy draft. The draft was the only drag on my time for this trip, and the first leg was the longest, so now the rest of the trip would be much more relaxed.

It felt great to have all the stressful parts of the trip behind me. I said a small prayer of thanks for making it safely to the hotel and for having had such a great ride. Too tired to get up and shower, I lay back on the bed, turned on the television, and drifted asleep with a smile on my face that mirrored the little boy's smile from Prague. What a phenomenal day!

Chapter 11
ZAGREB–SAN MARINO
4 SEPTEMBER 2016

I woke up feeling great! I lay in bed, reliving the prior day's events: I completed the single longest day of riding, went to an awesome Harley Davidson motorcycle rally, rode in beautiful weather the entire day, knocked Slovenia off of one list and added it to another, and I had a decent draft for my fantasy football league. All in all, a great "first" day of leave.

Had I not covered so much ground on Friday, I wouldn't have made it to Zagreb last night. I was incredibly grateful for how this trip was unfolding. The ride today would be much shorter, with a new definition of scenic. Today would see me collect two more countries on the bike, one of which is one of the world's tiniest, San Marino (fifth smallest by area, to be exact). I would also have the opportunity to ride down the western coastline of the Adriatic Sea.

I was in no rush today, so I took my time getting up. I took a shower and let the hot water wash away the sleepiness from my eyes and the weariness from my bones. I set aside my clothes for the trip and then packed the rest of my gear. Finally, I got dressed, donning every bit of heavy gear I had for protection. Once I completed my last check of the room to make sure I hadn't left anything behind, I made my way to the reception desk.

After checking out, I secured my gear to the bike and then returned to the hotel restaurant to eat breakfast. I could see my bike from where I sat, so I wasn't worried about anything happening to my bag. There were a few other riders also eating breakfast. I could see their bikes parked next to mine; they must've arrived later on last night. It looked as if they were on a long-distance trip of their own.

As I sat to eat, they were finishing up and proceeding outside to their bikes. I watched as they took their time getting everything packed up and squared away for the road. After a bit, they took off, and I picked up my phone to browse the Internet; not even a hint of any sense of urgency to hit the road. As I finished my meal, I messaged Glo to let her know that I was headed out. With the time zone difference, I was sure she was still fast asleep. Upon tapping the "Send" button, I took a final swig of my water and one of my coffee before pushing back from the table. Before heading out to the highway, I gassed up at a station around the corner from the hotel, and then I put my wheels to the pavement—it was time to hit the road.

Riding on a Sunday morning had some serious perks, or maybe just one big perk. There was virtually no traffic on the roads when I left, so it was a breeze following my GPS back to the highway, which would take me through some amazing views en route to my final destination for the day—San Marino.

San Marino is a beautiful area, with stunning hilly views surrounding the landlocked island nation. San Marino's history is as long as most other European countries. When the kingdoms in what is present-day Italy unified, San Marino was the only kingdom allowed to maintain its sovereignty.

I had to double-back a little ways through Croatia after leaving Zagreb to cut back through Slovenia. I didn't mind, as it was another beautiful day and I'd get a chance to see more of Slovenia. But I hit some pretty egregious lines at the border crossing into Slovenia—and there was no lane-splitting this time—so I had to wait like everyone else.

After about a 30-minute wait, I crossed the border back into Slovenia and enjoyed a nice-and-easy cruise. I decided to keep the thoughts mingling in my mind nice and light for now, batting away any serious thoughts that attempted to take over the white space. When I tell you that riding is therapeutic, I mean it has mental and spiritual cleansing abilities. However, it's physically taxing—but they have massage therapy for that. I basked in the sun, feeling the fresh warmth on my face. I couldn't have asked for a more relaxing or scenic ride.

I came up to Ljubljana, the capital city of Slovenia. The highway went around the outskirts of the city, so I avoided any through traffic. I didn't stop in town, but I thought to myself that I did want to come back for a more thorough visit. The town had some cool sights, and Castle Bled was just north of the city. There is something special about Slovenia, and I was going to come back to investigate, maybe to look for retirement property—I got the same "Home" vibe that I'd felt in Copenhagen.

I stopped to gas up right after passing Ljubljana. The break wasn't long—the Italian border was not too far, and I was itching to put another country notch on my belt. I had the hotel from San Marino as the destination in my GPS, and it wanted to take me on the quickest route—through the city of Bologna, off the major highway. To force the GPS onto the route I wanted to take, I plugged in an extra stop, a coastal town called Chioggia (just on the other side of Venice).

I was so excited to ride the coastal road; I remember how beautiful it was from the car when Glo and I had driven down the Croatian coastline. Back at the hotel in Zagreb, I played with the Garmin camera, feeling out the controls and memorizing the manual operations. The remote controls from the GPS panel were finicky, working on and off. Because the remote controls were so unreliable, I learned how to manually operate the camera blindly, using only touch. It didn't take long, as there were just a few buttons on the camera itself. I didn't want to miss the coastal views that lay ahead.

After crossing the Italian border, I was immediately faced with two realities. First, it was a ridiculously short ride to Venice. By my calculations, it would take a little more than an hour to pass the city. Second, just after crossing the border, the drivers became almost instantly more aggressive. I was terrified! Having ridden all over Europe at this point, I can say without a doubt that Italy had the scariest drivers. I was constantly on guard. It was normal to see cars weaving in and out of traffic, changing lanes with no signals, and straddling the lanes so that you couldn't pass them while they were deciding which lane was moving faster.

It took a little bit to adjust to the new style of highway driving, but after a while, I grew accustomed to it. I became more comfortable, but I also maintained a large distance between me and the cars in front. I spent so much time focusing on the cars and crazy drivers around me that I almost missed the exit for Venice. According to my GPS, I just had a little more to go before I turned off onto the small coastal highway.

Once I got onto the smaller one-lane highway that hugged the coast, I waited a bit before turning on the camera. I wanted to be ready to catch the amazing views afforded by this road without draining the battery. I rode past Chioggia, which was across a bridge. I almost began filming then, but I waited—I didn't want to waste battery life on the small views.

Shortly after passing Chioggia, I stopped off for fuel and lunch. The gas station was unmanned and self-serve only on Sundays. I was a little nervous, unsure if I'd have issues with operating the pump. Turned out it was easy enough, and soon I was pulling up to a McDonald's to eat. I grabbed my food and stood at the window table to eat, stretching out my back and butt.

While I ate, I contemplated how far I already was down this coastal highway and I still hadn't seen the sea.

I could smell it, and every once in a blue moon, I could catch a quick glimpse through the trees. But, compared to my expectations, this stretch was severely disappointing. The main issue was all the tall trees blocking the view of the coast. I had to wonder if that was on purpose—maybe there was a reason for all the tall and thick trees lining the highway. I held out hope that the view would open up soon, but I wasn't going to burn the battery life in the camera just to wait for the view that may never come. Back at the bike, I did a final stretch before hopping back on for what should have been the final stretch before I reached my hotel in San Marino.

Back on the coastal road, I soon came to accept that the coveted sea view was only for the trees that were blocking *my* view. This was the closest I could possibly get my bike to the sea without taking it on the grass, rocks, and sand. I decided to turn my focus on getting to San Marino rather than on what I couldn't see. The ride was still very enjoyable, and the weather was still all sun, so I had much for which to be grateful, despite my disappointment.

The further south I rode, the more congested the traffic became. Usually, congestion on the road wouldn't be a big deal for a biker, but it was also becoming more difficult to pass traffic because I was on a one-lane road with traffic going both ways. I could feel my spirits start to spiral downward. After all, I took the long way around so I could see the coastline, and all I could see was trees, and now, growing, insurmountable traffic. I decided then that I would refuse to sulk while on this amazing journey, especially about something so trivial. This was a once-in-a-lifetime opportunity, and I was going to appreciate *all* of it. I wasn't going to spend time feeling sorry for myself, or as my mom would call it, throwing myself a pity party.

As if the gods of traffic and motor vehicles heard my declaration, the congestion began to clear, allowing me to roll back on my throttle toward San Marino. Earlier this year, Glo and I had been down around this area; I took her to Venice for their Carnival (Carnevale di Venezia). She mentioned when we first arrived in Belgium that attending the Carnival of Venice was high on her list of things to experience. It almost didn't happen, because she started getting a little burned out while traveling. She actually told me that she didn't want to go; she assured me that she'd be fine if I went alone. I wasn't buying it, however, and after a time, she admitted that later on she would seriously regret not going. And so, we hopped on a plane for Venice.

While in Venice, we took a day to grab a train to the town of Rimini, and from there we made our way to San Marino by bus. I was riding past Rimini, so it made

ZAGREB–SAN MARINO

me think about the time that we'd spent there. After we finished hanging out in San Marino, we jumped on the bus back to Rimini so we could catch the train back to Venice.

On our trip, Glo and I had a lot of time to kill, so we walked all over the town, including the major tourist/shopping area. We stopped in a nail salon because they had the tanks in which you dipped your feet, and the fish would nibble at the dead skin on your feet. Neither of us had tried it before, so in the spirit of adventure, we took off our smelly shoes and socks and shoved our stinky feet into the tanks. We both laughed and giggled as the fish had their feast. It took the sensation of ticklishness to an all-new level for us both. That ended up being a great trip—especially for Glo, she really loved Venice and seeing all of the Carnival costumes and masks. I'm sure she would've seriously regretted not going.

Soon after passing Rimini, I turned onto the highway that would carry me to San Marino. As I rode, I was treated to spectacular visions of the rolling hills painted in a dusky light. It made for picturesque views, to be sure. I turned on the camera, determined to capture something of value today. I wasn't sure how much battery was left, but I hoped it would be enough for this portion of the ride. I didn't bother turning it off, opting instead to let whatever was left of the battery run out.

I climbed up the twisting and winding roads toward the fortified city of San Marino at the top of a massive hill. For this visit, I spent the extra bucks to get a room in a hotel at the very top of this hill, within the walls of the city. So, KB and I had to work for that view. I took the path toward the hotel at a very comfortable pace, but even then it was nerve-wracking. The steep and sharp curves on one-lane roads with oncoming traffic whipping around the bends were both terrifying and exhilarating.

With each steep slope climbed and sharp curve taken, I became much more comfortable handling the bike. I never left the pavement, but because of the trickiness of the ride, I began envisioning myself on a dirt bike—manhandling it to get it to do what I wanted. I could see the lights at the top of the hill getting closer with each switchback conquered, and before long I was pulling through the gates to the city itself.

I rode around the fortified town, reminiscing about our previous adventures here, as I searched for my hotel. Fifteen minutes after entering the city, I spotted it and parked in front to go check in. I informed the receptionist that I'd parked on the street, and she told me I'd need to move it to the garage after I finished checking in.

As the receptionist clacked away on her keyboard, I asked her if the room I booked had amazing views. Without batting an eye, she informed me that no, it did not. Then, after about 30 seconds, she looked up at me, smiled, and said, "It does now." I couldn't help but laugh—the cheesiness of it—after all, that's my kind of humor. I thanked her, and she directed me to the parking garage around the corner.

Back on the bike, I came upon the sign for the hotel parking garage, which was underground, behind a drop arm. I hit the buzzer, and a faint voice drifted over the intercom, "Yes?" I let her know I had found the parking garage and, without another word, up came the drop arm, and down the embankment I rode. I followed a gentleman all the way to the back of the garage, near the elevators that led to the hotel lobby. The parking situation was cramped to say the least, and because I was hitting the road early in the morning, I began to worry that I could be blocked in when it was time to leave. I found a spot that would be easy to get out of in the morning and backed KB in. I shut my bike down and grabbed my bag.

The hotel was really nice. It had a classy, antique vibe to it, as if it had played host to many important people in the past. I'm sure it had a very interesting history; I was just too tired to dig it up. I lugged all my stuff to my room and plopped it all on the floor.

I asked for a room with a view, and the receptionist did not disappoint! Opening the curtains, I had tear-inducing views of rolling hills dotted with small farm plots. The sun was setting, painting the entire scene with a beautiful orange glow. I stood outside on the balcony, taking pictures with my phone and soaking in the view. I wasn't in a rush to leave *this* scene, so I took a seat and texted a couple of the pictures I took on my phone to Glo to let her know I had arrived.

I thought about the trip getting here, realizing that it had taken a little longer than I thought it would. And while I'd had some disappointments on the road, I refused to let them be the highlight of my day. After washing the scene from the hotel balcony over with my eyes and thoughts once more, I decided to eat—the hunger in my gut decided it was the top priority now.

I made my way down to the reception desk and asked about any good restaurants nearby. She gave me the typical tourist response—and I was directed to a pricey Michelin-rated eatery around the corner. I decided to sit outside to enjoy the views of the setting sun, which seemed to be taking an extraordinarily long time to go down.

I ordered a pasta dish that appeared to be more for show than for eating. It was good, but there was an artsy quality to it—ergo, a scarcity of food on the plate. After the delicious, yet portion-challenged meal, I had more than enough room for dessert. I spied crème brûlée on the menu, and my spirits soared. It was easily one of my favorite desserts, and I was going to end the night with spoonfuls of creamy delight.

The waiter could see my excitement, and I think it was a little contagious (he seemed excited for me!)—which made what happened next all the more disappointing. He served up some sort of artistic version of crème brûlée, one with which I could've done without. It was a brûlée cake concoction, and as I laid my eyes on it, my heart sank. I just wanted normal crème brûlée, not a Picasso masterpiece. I thanked him—for the meal—and nibbled the dessert to completion. After paying the bill, he asked how the meal was, and I was honest: it was delicious but not filling enough, and the dessert was a little too artsy for me. He laughed and patted my shoulder as if sympathizing with my conflicted experience.

After dinner, I meandered through the corridors of the city, looking into shop windows and down stony corridors. Most shops were closed for the night but ready to spring open in the morning for business. In the darkness of night, I made my way back to my room. I peeled off the many layers of clothes and jumped into the shower. I was more tired than I expected to be, considering the easy day I'd had. Maybe it was my body feeling the effects of the accumulation of riding days. After my shower, I crashed into the bed and shot a quick text to Glo, wishing her a great day; then before I knew it, I was drifting off to the land of the Sandman.

Chapter 12
SAN MARINO–LÖRRACH
5 SEPTEMBER 2016

I woke up more sore than I'd ever been during the trip; physically, I could feel the trip starting to take its toll on me. I got in a good stretch, just to loosen up the muscles a little. Today I wanted to hit the road fairly early, so last night I had set an alarm. Because it was Monday, I knew I could expect to hit traffic at some point, but I wanted to get ahead of the morning rush hour as much as possible. Today began the return trek home, and I was ready for it.

I was really excited to ride through the Swiss Alps again. For that reason, it was going to be the most important video day, so this time, with my brand new action camera with which to capture the majestic qualities of the beautiful mountains—I made sure to charge the camera last night. At most, I should expect the battery to last for two hours, but it seemed to drain much faster. Therefore, I needed to be extra judicious with how I used it. One slip-up and I could drain the entire battery without knowing it.

With a little extra time on my hands, I practiced with the camera again, feeling out the curves and contours of the device with my eyes closed. I fingered the buttons and levers, cementing each of their functions and locations in my mind. As I unplugged the camera to place it in the bag, I checked it again to make sure it was fully charged, and once I was satisfied, I put it in the bag and zipped it up.

With everything packed and ready, I finished my morning routine—cleaning my teeth, face, and pits—and geared up. Because I was leaving so early, there'd be no breakfast at the hotel today; I'd have to get it on the road during a stop.

After I checked out, I made my way down to the tiny garage. I hoped KB wasn't blocked in (as were some of the other vehicles on my way in the day before). The elevator doors opened; I stepped out, walked down the short hallway toward the garage, and was relieved to

SAN MARINO–LÖRRACH

see KB free and clear of any vehicular obstacles. After loading up my gear and setting my GPS for Gate 32 Harley Davidson in Milan, Italy, I pulled out into the crisp and early morning air.

The early morning light played across the rolling hills that were covered with a thin layer of fog, creating pockets of shadows across the land—this scene was simply gorgeous. I decided to sacrifice some of my battery charge on my camera to capture part of my ride down the large hill from San Marino toward the highway that would take me to Milan. The sun was only just rising, so KB and I drank in the light of dawn while we ate the kilometers down the hill.

With very little traffic for a Monday morning, I navigated my way down the windy paths and roads toward the major highway I had avoided yesterday. The closer to the highway I got, the more the traffic picked up, and before long I was on the highway headed north toward Bologna. This was a straight shot to my first stop of the day, the Harley shop in Milan, so I took comfort in that I didn't need to focus on directions so much as the traffic around me. I kept my mind sharp and focused on the traffic rather than getting distracted with nonpertinent thoughts. I hit pockets of rush-hour traffic as people were up and starting their lives for the day.

I thought my introduction to riding in Italy yesterday was nerve-wracking; I was sorely mistaken—I've never been more terrified on my bike than when riding in the thick of Italian rush-hour traffic. The drivers here are CRAZY on the road! Really, it was more of the same, as when I'd entered the country initially; however, with heavier traffic and people rushing to get to work, it felt like the perceived transgressions were even more outrageous. Because I couldn't predict people's actions on the road due to everyone's erratic driving patterns, I had a hard time passing vehicles out of fear that I'd get hit. I'm not sure I've ever been more focused riding on dry roads.

Once I hit a pocket clear of traffic, I made a stop to gas up and eat breakfast. I was about 45 minutes outside the town of Bologna, so I wanted to stop while I could before I hit more traffic. The huge rest stop I pulled into looked to have everything I needed. I love the rest stops in Europe—they're clean, seemingly safe, and usually have really good food.

I fueled up first and then rode to the restaurant side of the complex. I decided to leave my roll bag attached to the bike. I was going to test the safety factor of my rest-stop theory, mostly because I just didn't feel like going through the motions of unstrapping/restrapping the bag. I did lock the front forks in place and took my

SAN MARINO–LÖRRACH

camera off the handle bars. I slipped the camera into my pocket and made my way into the restaurant.

I stood in line to what appeared to be a legit bakery. I ordered a *croque monsieur* (a type of sandwich) and an Americano coffee. Funny story about the Americano—many places around Europe take their coffee very seriously, so they use as little water as possible. This means that the coffee tends to be much thicker and a lot stronger than the coffee we drink in the States. The Americano coffee is aptly named because once the barista makes a normal coffee, they add a ton of hot water (which waters down the coffee quite a bit) to make the Americano. I've ordered coffee in places where they made fun of the severely watered-down coffee we drink in the U.S. Here in Italy, from what I've observed, the Americano is considered gross, and it's only on most menus for tourists with weak palates. Well, paint my palate weak as hell, because I love the Americano! For me, it has all the flavor of the delicious coffee beans they used without feeling like I was drinking something with the consistency of mud.

Because I'd left my bag on the bike, I didn't want to linger out of view of KB longer than necessary. I scarfed down the food and coffee, then jumped back on the bike. Back on the highway, I passed through Bologna with next-to-no traffic. Rush hour was done for now, so I was able to fly through the town. Because I was still dealing with these unpredictable motorists, I maintained my focus on the road, not letting my mind wander. The time seemed to drag on as I made my way toward Milan, probably due to the amount of focus I was spending on the vehicles around me. After another gas break about 60 minutes away from the Harley shop, I was back on the road, eager to close out the distance to my first main stop for the day.

With light traffic, I finally hit Milan at just under an hour. The Harley dealership was tucked in a small suburban area, a decent ways away from the city center. For that, I was thankful—it meant a lot less congestion as I navigated to and from the dealership. After looping around the block looking for the entrance and a place to park, I found a spot and pulled in. Gingerly, I hopped off the bike and took in a big and refreshing stretch. I grabbed a bottle of water from my roll bag and took a swig; I needed to remember to stay hydrated. Staying hydrated was tough because it required a delicate balance: on the one hand, if you drank too much, you'd be hydrated but have to stop every ten minutes to piss. On the other, becoming dehydrated on the road could lead to serious muscle cramps, severe headaches, and reduced stamina. So far, I felt pretty good, but I needed to keep an eye on my body's hydration.

SAN MARINO–LÖRRACH

After packing the water bottle back into my bag, I walked into the store. Considering it was on the outskirts of the city, the inside was very spacious. I walked around, browsing everything from parts and services to T-shirts and jackets. Eventually, I found a T-shirt for myself and one for Glo, and a pin and patch.

The sales associate was very nice and talkative. We chatted a little bit about her life and my ongoing trip. After she rang up my purchases, she put some extra swag from the store in my bag—a couple of store ballpoint pens and an extra pin. After I paid, she pointed me to the coffee machine and the bathroom. I could most definitely use a boost to my energy levels; I was beginning to drag, and I was only about at the halfway point of the ride for the day.

Before I sat down to relax, I went back outside, retrieved my camera and charging cables, and returned, selecting a booth to set my stuff down. I plugged in my phone and camera to get a little extra charge in both before I hit the road again—the border crossing was near, and I wouldn't get another opportunity to charge my camera. I got my coffee from the vending machine and then plopped down in the booth.

While sipping on my warm coffee and letting my equipment charge, I played on my phone for a bit. I also messaged Glo to see how she was doing and to let her know I was on the return leg of my trip. She was up and, at the moment, not busy, so we chatted for a bit. She told me about my mom's recovery and some of the struggles she was having. My mom was givin' her all during her recovery; sometimes overdoing it. She really wanted to be healed—and quickly. I could understand; my mom is a very independent woman, so having to depend on another for so long can be tough.

Other than discussing my mom's recovery, the conversation stayed pretty surface-level. My stepsister had gone to California to visit my Mom, and she and Glo are pretty close. So they got to hang out, hit the LA county fair, went shopping, and on and on—I was glad that she was getting some down time to enjoy California in the summer. I could tell that Glo was really ready to come home, though; she sounded tired. I let her know, again, how much I truly appreciated her willingness to spend two months helping my mom rehab her knees. My mom told me how incredible Glo was, helping her through the rigorous recovery—Glo was way more engaged with the process than my mom assumed she'd be. Who knows, this could be a calling for her in life, if she were so inclined.

Vocalizing my appreciation seemed to soften the wall that I assumed to be resentfulness, and she let me know that she missed me and missed being home. I

SAN MARINO–LÖRRACH ★

assured her that she would be home, in her own bed, before she knew it. With that, it was time to hit the road again. We said our goodbyes, and I downed the remaining coffee in my cup. I wrapped up my charging cables and grabbed my merchandise. Once everything was packed in my roll bag and the camera reinstalled in its brace, I stretched one final time before mounting KB.

Back on the bike, I set the destination for Lörrach, Germany, a town very close to Basel, Switzerland. This town was going to be my stopping point for the night, the last before the homestretch. I was already very close to the Swiss border, and riding through Switzerland wouldn't take long. I had about three to four hours left on the road—an easy day for sure.

Before pulling out of the parking lot, I double-checked the camera to make sure it was at a good angle to catch the upcoming views of the Alps. I chose not to stop for gas before getting back on the highway because I'd need to stop after the border anyway to grab another vehicle pass.

Back on the road, I rolled past Como, a lake town near Ghedi Air Base (an Italian Air Force base). I had a couple of friends stationed there, but neither were available to grab a bite, so I rolled on. Funny enough, both of them are in the fantasy football league for which we drafted a couple of nights ago—small world.

In no time, I came up to the Swiss border. Shortly after crossing, I quickly stopped for a vehicle pass and some gas. This time, I put the vehicle pass on the windshield because Switzerland uses a network of cameras along the highway that scans the pass on the cars as they drive by. Without the pass on the windshield, I could expect to get tickets in the mail. And, from what I've heard, tickets from Switzerland were insanely expensive.

With a full tank and my pass, I triple-checked my camera one last time. I really wanted to get the money shot of the mountains on such a clear and beautiful day. Once I was certain that the angle of the dangle was good (I hung my camera down from the handlebars) and checked my camera controls, I pulled out of the station onto the highway and waited for the beautiful scene to reveal itself before me. This is what I had been waiting to capture—the Adriatic coastline video didn't pan out as I'd hoped, so I was doubly excited because it was such a nice day. I was in a light mood and ready to see some amazing things.

As I hit the road, I had a familiar sense of appreciation for being in a position to enjoy something so crazy as a 15-country motorcycle ride. How many people in the world would have this kind of opportunity? Not many—therefore, I felt compelled to take advantage of my unique opportunity.

SAN MARINO–LÖRRACH

As I rode, waiting for the massive mountains to come into view, I began to think about my promotion situation. I'd busted my ass to prove that I was worthy of the "Definitely Promote" endorsement on my second go at this promotion process. I'm not sure why I didn't receive one, but it was disappointing. With no "Definitely Promote" endorsement, I didn't stand much of a chance for my second try at promoting to Major. Plus, all the work my mentors and I had put into my promotion package had been kicked to the curb by the base commander, who wrote a very unusual package. Don't get me wrong—I was very grateful that he took the time to do so—but I wasn't confident that it would stand out in the way he had hoped. I'm very confident the supplemental promotion board that met this past June will find me worthy to promote, so most of this mental commotion should be a moot point.

The whole ordeal was incredibly stressful and embarrassing, and I want nothing more than for it to be over. I could feel the creep of doubt and negativity begin to invade my mind, latching on and taking root. As I opened the door to the self-pity party, I could see the dark void of angry and hurt emotions swirling around, inviting me to step over the threshold and into the mental muck. I closed the door and turned around; I chose to face the sunshine and blue skies on this blessed ride through the Alps.

Because I was about to see something amazing—the Alps opening up to me like a gigantic birthday present—I refused to let my promotion situation or tepid marriage dilute this particular experience. I cleared my thoughts, cranked up my music, and leaned into the wind whipping past my windshield. Smiling, I could feel positive energy begin to flow through me. This was the choice I'd made—and I knew I'd chosen most wisely.

Soon enough, I began to see the mountains begin to peek around the curves. Excited, I flipped the camera on and began recording. All I could do was hope is that it was working as intended. As I rounded a gentle curve, the Alps fully came alive. The snowcapped peaks cut jagged lines against the bright blue sky. The mountains loomed as large as titans in front of me. The gray-colored rock formations were dotted with green vegetation, thicker at the base and growing more sparse the higher up the mountainside it climbed.

I couldn't pull my eyes away from the stunning scene before me. I could stare at that scene all day, every day. It amazed me that something this beautiful existed. I knew then that this is what I wanted to look at every day for the rest of my life. The sun gleamed off the white caps, as if to emphasize the fact that these mountains were so large, those snowcaps would take a lot more than a warm summer to melt. They were a permanent

SAN MARINO–LÖRRACH ★

fixture of beauty. I glided around traffic, capturing all I could with both the camera on the bike and the camera in my mind. When I retire, if I could settle somewhere with half of this view, I would live and die happy. As I continued along the large, sweeping curves of the highway, the views began to dull a bit, so I turned off my camera. Thankful for this experience, I pressed down the road, rolling on the throttle and closing in on my final stop for the night.

The road was pretty clear for quite a while, allowing me to have few cares in the world surrounded by the intense natural beauty. I pulled off to fuel up and stretch one final time before heading to Lörrach. I felt full of energy fresh off the road, so I didn't bother getting a coffee. After fueling up, I walked around the store in the gas station for a bit, focusing on stretching out my glutes while looking at the various souvenirs on the racks. After a good and long stretch, I jumped back on KB and made my way back to the highway.

It wasn't long before I ran into a construction-caused traffic jam (bumper to bumper). Sitting there in traffic, I suddenly had a great idea! I flipped my camera back on and began splitting the lanes. I was much more comfortable splitting lanes with more experience under my belt, understanding the flow and expectation of the traffic around me. I thought it'd be cool to see what splitting lanes actually looked like on video, so I recorded my "Splitting the lanes" adventure.

Traffic was backed up for quite a distance, but splitting the lanes got me through it all in about 15 minutes. Once I got ahead of the traffic, I turned off the camera, excited to watch the footage later on. With the congestion behind me, I began to see some dark clouds lurking ahead. To this point I had been blessed with supremely mild weather. However, mountain forecasting can be tricky, and if you're not careful, inclement weather could quickly sneak up on you and do some damage.

I continued riding until I came to a long tunnel. Before leaving the cover of the tunnel, I pulled off to the side and put the rain cover over my roll bag. Just beyond the tunnel exit, I could see the dark skies ahead, waiting for me, promising to rain and make my going a little tougher. I debated whether to don my rain gear, but ultimately, I decided against it. The rain gear is very uncomfortable, and I don't like wearing it unless I absolutely have to. I still get nervous that my pant leg will melt to the bike, so there are times when I'll risk the weather without it. This was going to be one of those times. Once my gear was secured, I hopped back on the bike and pulled back onto the road.

Before long, it began to sprinkle. Nothing crazy, but enough to cause me to doubt my decision to leave my rain gear in the bag. Construction was heavy on my side of the highway, so I continued to hit spots of congestion. Finally, the construction ended, and I hit the open road again.

I was stoked that I was no longer hindered by traffic and just waited for what I hoped would be a break in the rain and gray skies. As if the sun had heard my plea, the gray clouds began to part, giving way to blue skies once again. The further on I rode, the drier the road and the more fully the sun climbed out from behind the gray cover. No longer riding in wet conditions, I was back on dry pavement and incredibly close to the Swiss/German border. I cranked up my tunes and rolled back on the throttle.

I arrived at the border, which was somewhat run-down looking, but I pressed on, not having to stop for any checks. I was really close to the town of Basel, Switzerland, and shortly after crossing into Germany, I was in the town of Lörrach. I'd made it to my last overnight stop on the long road home!

Looking for my hotel, I got all kinds of lost. My GPS led me down a dead-end residential street, apparently inhabited by clouds of bees. I was able to ask a random pedestrian for directions to my hotel *and* avoid getting stung. With my skin crawling from the inordinate number of bees, I pulled out of the neighborhood and looped around the corner to my hotel; turns out, it wasn't very far at all from where Mr. GPS took me.

With no private parking, I double-checked the locks on my bike and detached everything of importance. The area seemed a bit run down, so I was a little nervous about leaving my bike out in the open. The hotel was attached to a small and seedy-looking strip mall, so I had my head on a swivel. Check-in was easy and I lugged my gear up the flight of stairs to my room. Though small and stuffy, I realized that my room overlooked the parking lot, so I could see my bike clear as day, which made me feel much better about the parking situation. Otherwise, I might have been compelled to periodically go outside to check on it.

I messaged Glo to let her know I had arrived and then relaxed for a bit before dinner. Any warmth from our previous conversation earlier that day was gone—communication with Glo was back to being strained. There is no affection between us right now, which makes our relationship as cold as ice. The physical separation makes it easier for me to deal with it, though I'm willing to bet that it is doing the opposite for her.

Being a solitary soul works wonders to keep my stress down. I was recently told that introverts usually recharge their batteries when they're alone, and while I have no idea how true that was in general, I knew it was true for me. I expected that by the time Glo came home, I'd be in a much better mental and spiritual place to deal with our issues. I doubt it would be as easy for her—in fact, I'd bet money on it.

After a bit, I decided to grab a bite to eat. There was a Chinese restaurant next door, so tonight was going to be dinner a la Chinese cuisine. I made my way to the restaurant, not even bothering to ask the hotel receptionist about any good places around to eat because I had no intention of riding anywhere else for the rest of the night anyway.

I brought my travel journal and wrote while I ate; I had a lot of writing to catch up on. I was so far behind on recounting my tales of travel but was determined to complete each journey in the journal. The food was pretty good, but the star of the show was the jasmine tea. I could've drunk that all night (though I'd have never left the bathroom).

After dinner, I made my way back to the room, checking on my bike on the way. Finally in the room for the night, I climbed out of my gear and under the waiting bed covers. I tried to write more in my journal, taking advantage of every drop of wakefulness I could. This was the last night I was going to sleep in a bed other than my own for a while. Before long, I could feel myself dozing off, the journal and pen sliding out of my hands. I had enough wherewithal to put the journal on the night stand so that I didn't make any more stray marks on the page. Then, I drifted away, letting the embrace of sleep wrap me up. Last day of the ride would be tomorrow!

Chapter 13

LÖRRACH–HOME
6 SEPTEMBER 2016

"HOME STRETCH!" was the first thought that popped into my head when I awoke. Because yesterday's ride was so much shorter than most other rides so far, I'd actually arrived in town early in the evening—meaning, I got to bed pretty early. I woke up well rested and ready to rock 'n' roll. I rolled out of bed and got in a good long stretch; I was excited to hit the road extra early today. Don't get me wrong—I was having a blast on this trip—but I was ready to pull into my garage, feeling accomplished and complete.

Within 15 minutes of opening my eyes, I was downstairs handing over my room key and completing checkout. I strapped my roll bag to the luggage rack and wiped some of the condensation off KB. The air was cool, as the sun was still fairly low on the horizon. Once I'd dried the seat and tank as much as I could, I cranked KB up and set my GPS.

With the Luxembourg Harley-Davidson dealership set as my next destination, I rolled out of the parking lot, looking to gas up. I was able to navigate the roads around Lörrach without having to bother with any traffic. I stopped on the edge of town to fuel up and get in a final deep stretch. With no breakfast in my stomach, I would've at least grabbed a cup of coffee, but the station was closed. So, I was left to use the automatic gas pump and leave. The lack of coffee and breakfast just gave me something to look forward to after I'd made some headway on the road. With the sun still climbing out of its slumber, I pulled out of the gas station and onto the road for the home stretch.

It wasn't long before I was pulling onto the on ramp toward the highway. As I settled into my ride, I began to take account of my surroundings. The morning light cast a lot of pinks and oranges over the lush, if not overgrown, vegetation around the highway. This light was oddly beautiful, almost magical. Searching the archives

LÖRRACH-HOME

of my mind for something to compare this sight to, the best I could do was to think of the lighting in a dream sequence from a fantasy movie.

I continued to be drawn to the weird light of the morning all around me as it cast a soft glow over everything it touched. All the distinguishing lines that separated one tree from another, or the base of a street lamp from the concrete around it, was soft and fuzzy. There were no sharp contrasts. Even though I was in the present, on the road and passing an occasional truck, my mind was occupied with this strangely intense light. What was it that made the soft glow feel so inviting? This was new to me, and I was absolutely captivated, feeling as if I were in a lucid dream. The ride seemed to stretch for a while (time probably elongated by the weird *Twilight Zone* light I was experiencing), and then I came up to the German/French border. It surprised me that I had made it to the border so quickly, but more than likely, time just slipped by as I was admiring the visual effect of the light around me.

As I crossed out of Germany and into France, the light suddenly changed—it became suddenly much more harsh. The defining lines around the trees and the fixed structures on the road seemed to be much sharper and detailed. I take that back—it wasn't that the light was now harsh—rather, the light appeared normal, which was harsh in comparison to what I'd just experienced. The sun's hue had lost its magic as it rose higher in the sky when I crossed into France. I wasn't really sure what just happened—or how to explain it—but I can say it was a very positive and warm experience—not a hint of danger or threat. I can only hope that I get to experience that sight again—it was indeed magical.

Soon after crossing the border into France, I arrived at the city of Strasbourg. Although it was still early, it seemed the right time for the early birds to be up and moving about the city. I needed to change highways, which meant having to drive through the city center, hitting a little traffic. Driving through Strasbourg, I could tell it was an old town, but very beautiful. I also knew they had a Harley Davidson store here, but it was way too early for them to be open, so I had a little extra incentive to come back for a visit.

While in traffic, I had a chance to consider—and get excited about—the fact that I was one country away from hitting the 15th of the trip. I could now officially cross France off the list of 20 and, within a couple more hours on the road, I would be crossing the border into Luxembourg, country number 18 out of 20. I was really excited, because this goal now seemed completely achievable. I'd been a bit nervous about setting a goal of 20, because the number might have been too high and unattainable. Now, three (soon to be two) countries away, it didn't seem so crazy.

I navigated the streets of Strasbourg and, before long, I was back on the highway. Once I exited the city, I could see I was running low on gas—both in the tank and in my belly. I still hadn't had anything to eat or coffee to drink, and that was about to change. As the city faded from sight in my rearview mirror, I turned my attention to the road ahead and more urgently, food and gas ahead.

About 20 minutes outside the city, I pulled into a little gas station/restaurant. It wasn't a large rest stop like others I've stopped at, but it was clean—and they had food. First I gassed up, and then I pulled into the parking area for the restaurant. I left my roll bag on the bike; it was so rural out here, I couldn't imagine anything happening to it. I ordered a coffee and a breakfast pastry. It wasn't much to eat, but I wanted to avoid feeling too full on the road, so it was enough to satiate my hunger. I grabbed a high table at the window facing my bike and stood while I ate and drank, fueling my own tank.

After the quick meal, I walked back to the bike and stretched out my legs as much as I could. After a final big stretch, I hopped on KB, cranked the engine, and pulled out of the rest stop. The sun shone high and bright in the blue sky, dotted with the occasional lazy cloud. As I got back on the highway, I relished the feeling of the sun on my face through the visor of my helmet. I pumped my music through the speakers in my helmet and cruised on, feeling really good.

My ride through the French countryside was free and clear of traffic. I couldn't help but smile at the great time I was making, as each kilometer marker I passed brought me one marker closer to home. I came up to and bypassed another large French town, Metz. The highway curved around this town, so I didn't have to drive through it. Metz also had a Harley Davidson shop, and while I did contemplate stopping, I looked at the time. I would have to wait about an hour for them to open, so I opted to just keep riding. Waiting wasn't the issue; I was just ready to get home. As planned, I would make it to the Harley Davidson in Luxembourg shortly after they opened, so I bypassed Metz and kept it moving to Luxembourg.

Luxembourg, the 28th smallest country in the world, is a great place to visit. The capital city, Luxembourg City, is surrounded by great views and has an amazing shopping district. There is also a phenomenal castle in the northern part of the country: Vianden Castle is high up on a hill overlooking the countryside surrounding it. I've been there twice—once by myself and another time with my dad when he came for a visit.

While I enjoy Luxembourg City, I've had a couple of irritating experiences that had put a bad taste in my mouth. Both negative experiences happened during my first visit to the country back in 2013. I took a weekend trip from Eindhoven in the Netherlands, where I was stationed for a six-month assignment. I was so excited to get the chance to explore that the first free weekend I had available I drove my rental car straight to Luxembourg. I enjoyed the city center, taking pictures of the architecture, statues, and some of the beautiful landscapes that the edge of the city overlooked.

Bad-taste incident #1: I saw a lady taking a picture of what I assumed was her boyfriend. I asked them, "Hey, would you like me to take a picture of the two of you together?" The guy immediately said "Yes" and "Thank you." The lady, however, slowly turned her head toward me, terror filling her eyes. She slowly shook her head repeatedly, saying, "No, no, no, no. . . ." It was a very weird scene. I immediately put my hands up in a nonthreatening gesture and backed away. It looked as if she were on the verge of screaming, and I wasn't even that close to her. I looked at the guy she was with, and he was looking at her, appearing just as confused as I felt. He looked at me and shrugged his shoulders, as if to say, "I'm sorry, Bro." I returned the shrug, turned on my heels, and left the scene. I felt devastated—I never had someone look at me the way she did. Her eyes said that she expected the absolute worst of me, and it stung deep. I had only offered to take a picture of them, but the way she reacted, I might as well had been brandishing a knife. I should've prefaced the story: I am very sensitive to events like that—maybe the same occurrence happening to someone else would've had a much different effect—but it really messed me up at the time.

Bad-taste incident #2 happened maybe 30 minutes later. Having finally shaken off the previous experience, I was walking around the shopping district, window-shopping. I stopped at the window of a home décor store, and peeked in. Obviously, I wasn't planning to buy any home décor, but the items in the store looked very unique, so I decided to go in and check it out—who knows, maybe I'd get some ideas for my house in Minot. I walked the entirety of the store, browsing the merchandise, and as I made my way toward the exit, I noticed that someone had tracked dog crap in the store. What a jerk! Who does that? I put on my Sherlock Holmes hat, and investigated the tracks, following them out the front door. As I exited, the tracks made a sharp right turn and ended at the window. There stood a large pile of dog crap, freshly marked with a big Timberland boot print. Looking at the bottom of my boot (also Timberland)—turns out, I was the culprit.

I was furious! Who lets their dog crap on the street without picking up after them?

I considered going back into the store and letting someone know what happened. But, I chose to succumb to my anger instead and just left the store in search of some way to clean my boot. I found a café with outdoor seating. I grabbed a seat and ordered a coffee. While drinking my warm drink, I worked to clean my boot. Finishing both the coffee and my boot-cleaning, I continued to walk the shopping beat, feeling guilty about leaving the trail of dog crap throughout that nice-looking store.

So, Luxembourg and I had a little bit of a history, but it wasn't going to stop me from hitting the only Harley Davidson shop in the country. I followed my GPS off the highway and onto a smaller county road. It was almost time for me to gas up again, but I planned to do so after visiting the Harley shop, which was definitely tucked away far from the major highway.

About 15 minutes from the highway, I spotted the store on the other side of some road construction. I cut across the traffic and parked the bike in front, dismounted, and got in a great big stretch. I popped into the store and walked around, looking at all the merchandise. I hit the T-shirt racks for something nice for Glo and myself. After grabbing a couple of shirts, I found a pin for my vest, but no patches. All of the staff seemed a bit preoccupied with other customers, so I didn't really chat with anyone—I paid for my merchandise and then grabbed a coffee.

After I'd stretched out and relaxed for a bit at the store's lounge area, it was time for KB and I to get back to work. I packed my purchases in my roll bag, brought KB roaring back to life, and pulled out into the construction zone, weaving and dodging orange cones. To get to the closest gas station, I had to pass underneath the highway. After filling up, I grabbed a new bottle of water (I'd run out of water on yesterday's ride, and my throat was already parched) and hit the road. With my GPS set for home, I backtracked to the highway and started on the final leg.

I couldn't believe I was about to complete such a huge trip! On the road with my music jamming, the enormity of this trip began to set in—I now had checked off 18 European countries on the back of my motorcycle, with only two left to conquer. I began mapping out the possibilities of capturing the last two before we were due to leave next summer.

Two very specific trip ideas began to take shape in my mind as I thought out adventures to match the challenge and intensity of the one I was about to complete. The first trip was a voyage through France and through

LÖRRACH–HOME ✭

the Chunnel to England. From there, I envisioned riding across southern England to Wales, and to the town of Barmouth, which is nestled in Snowdonia National Park on the coast. The area around Barmouth is said to be supremely gorgeous, so I could only imagine how it would look from behind my helmet visor. From Barmouth, I'd travel to a port and take the ferry to Ireland, most likely to Dublin. Once in Dublin, I could jump on the highway stretching due north, past Belfast and on to the Giant's Causeway (an area of natural rock formations caused by an ancient volcanic eruption) on the north coast of Ireland. I had previously visited Belfast but didn't have time to hit the Causeway, so I wouldn't want to miss out on it a second time.

After the Giant's Causeway, I'd ride back down to Belfast and take a ferry across the Irish Sea to the Isle of Man. It's supposed to be a very popular and famous motorcycle scene, boasting some pretty sweet race tracks. The next ferry would make port as close to Scotland as possible, and after a day's ride north into the Scottish highlands, my trek would turn homeward-bound.

That trip would be amazing and probably offer some very unique scenery that I had yet to see from my bike. I also knew that people would jump over themselves to join me on that trip. For some reason, people had no issues traveling to the English-speaking United Kingdom, but to suggest traveling somewhere that boasted a different language as the official language—people are quick to pump the brakes. Just an observation.

The second trip swirling in my mind involved riding down the center of France to Carcassonne and then crossing into Spain to get to Andorra. Earlier this year, Glo and I had flown to Madrid and met up with Angel and her boyfriend. We rented a car and traveled from Madrid to Pamplona, where I participated in the (in)famous bull run, and then on to the country of Andorra before finishing the road trip through the Pyrenees mountain range and down to Barcelona. While in Andorra, the 17th-smallest country in the world (a tiny, independent principality), I spotted a Harley Davidson dealership. It was an unexpected find, and I wish I had known about it so that I could've planned to be there while they were open. I'd love to get a shirt and a pin from that place. So, if I were to pull off this second trip, I would absolutely plan it around their opening hours.

From Andorra, the route would run through the south of France into the country of Monaco before turning north through Switzerland/France in the direction of home. For me, this trip was attractive because it included Andorra and Monaco, though I'd also check off Spain and get a great shot of my bike in front of the massive medieval fortified city of Carcassonne, France.

LÖRRACH–HOME

Either trip would give me what I needed—and more—to meet my "20 European countries on the bike" goal. The perfect plan, though, would really depend on the weather, as I would have to hope for a warm spring so that I could avoid having to deal with winter snow and ice. Fingers crossed, I could make one of these trips a reality; I was running out of options to make good on checking off the last two countries.

In the midst of my plotting and planning, I crossed the border into Belgium. I was getting close and could feel the excitement growing from within. Coming from Luxembourg, I entered the south of Belgium, which took me by the historic town of Bastogne, the Bastogne War Museum, and the Mardasson Memorial monument (of WWII's "Battle of the Bulge"). As I rode past the exit to the town, I reminisced about visiting the area. I'd been here twice before, touring the town, the Museum, the Mardasson Memorial, and the forests in which the famous Battle of the Bulge was fought. The Mardasson Memorial was a tribute to the American soldiers who'd fought and lost their lives at the Battle of the Bulge during the war.

The first time we visited, we had a local guide who took us to the forests near the town where the Battle of the Bulge was waged. Walking through the trees, we could still see the indentations of the foxholes the soldiers dug to hunker down during the fight, now covered with layers of leaves and other forest debris. It was easy to tell that people came out to clean the leaves and branches from the holes periodically. The scene was surreal; I imagined that wherever my footsteps fell, they were the same spots that soldiers fought, bled, froze, and died. I could barely imagine the treacherous conditions these soldiers had to endure. They couldn't know that the battle they were fighting at this very spot would become such a significant point in the war, stopping the German forces in their tracks. Both visits were incredible, and weighed heavy on the soul—heavy even still as I write these words.

Living in Europe has made me realize that there are WWII memorials and sites all over the place. The more I thought about it, the more I realized just how huge the Second World War really was. It touched every corner of the globe in one way or another, but so many of the brutal battles took place right here, in Europe, in so many places that I've already visited without much consideration to the war. It's a sobering topic and a shuddering thought, to be sure.

About an hour past Bastogne, I stopped one final time to gas up and grab dinner. I took my time eating at the restaurant by the station, stretching my back and glutes while enjoying the warm meal. After I put my tray and trash away, I got back to KB, and tiredly swung my leg over the seat.

This was it! But, the ride from the last stop to my driveway seemed to drag on. I tried to distract myself by thinking about everything from Glo to the upcoming fantasy football season—to no avail. I guess I would have to feel every ticking second of this last stretch. I cranked up my music and settled in to endure the remainder of the ride.

Luckily, I avoided any serious traffic, and, before long, I was pulling into my driveway. I rolled into the garage and cranked on the throttle twice before cutting the engine. It felt so good to be home! I slowly unwrapped my bag straps from the luggage rack, and shuffled toward the house, listening to the garage door slowly clink its way to the ground.

I walked through the door and dropped my gear on the front room floor, exhausted. Enwei was right there to greet me, eagerly reaching up to be picked up and petted. My trip was complete, and I was relieved and thankful all at once. After a prayer of thanks for the safe return, I walked to the laundry room, stripping off my gear along the way. It was still late afternoon, so I had time to relax before I had to start getting ready for work in the morning. I messaged Glo to let her know I'd made it home, and then dragged myself to the shower.

As I let the hot water hit my wary bones, I considered how much I've grown to love riding, even if my tailbone tells me it doesn't. I was glad to be home, but I was just as excited about the next trip—whenever and wherever that might be.

THE WINTER RIDE

Countries to Travel to:

- ★ ~~Belgium~~
- ★ ~~The Netherlands~~
- ★ ~~Germany~~
- ★ ~~Denmark~~
- ★ ~~Sweden~~
- ★ ~~Austria~~
- ★ ~~Liechtenstein~~
- ★ ~~Switzerland~~
- ★ ~~Poland~~
- ★ ~~Czech Republic~~
- ★ ~~Slovakia~~
- ★ ~~Hungary~~
- ★ ~~Slovenia~~
- ★ ~~Croatia~~
- ★ ~~Italy~~
- ★ ~~San Marino~~
- ★ ~~France~~
- ★ ~~Luxembourg~~
- ★ England (19 of 20)
- ★ Wales (20 of 20)

Miles/Kilometers Traveled: 944 mi/1,519 km

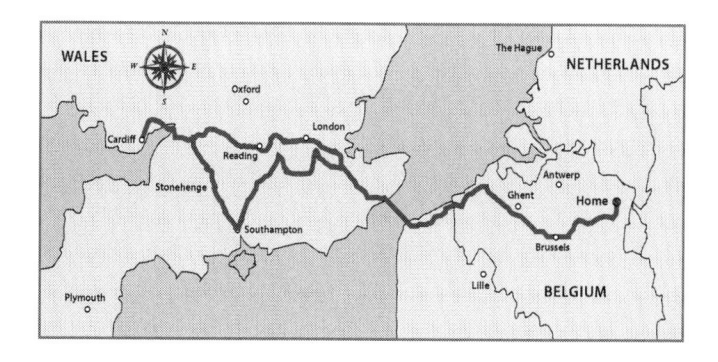

Chapter 14

PREPARATIONS
26 JANUARY 2017

Forget it—I'm doing it. I'm angry, hurt, frustrated, confused, and any other adjectives that can be used to describe where I am in life right now. I kept looking at the weather app for southern England and Wales, checking to make sure I wouldn't be hit with a surprise storm on my way to completing my motorcycle travel goal. I decided to collect my last two countries on my bike this weekend: England and Wales. Once I complete this journey, I'll have hit my 19th and 20th countries on the motorcycle, wrapping up the travel goal I set for myself last summer.

I already finished my first travel goal over the Thanksgiving holiday break with a road trip by car through Bulgaria, Serbia, Kosovo, Albania, and Macedonia with my friend James. It was phenomenal, and not only did I make a good friend, we happened upon a little hidden travel gem in the middle of Macedonia, the gorgeous lake town of Ohrid. Originally, I was supposed to complete the trip with Glo, but she backed out, afraid that the trip would be unsafe (she had her fair share of going to countries that didn't have the best of reputations)—after our trip to Belarus and Ukraine, she was a little travel-shy. Those trips ended fine, but there were definitely some disconcerting parts from each.

My intent was to finish out my motorcycle travel goal in late spring, just before we had to pack up and leave Belgium for my new assignment. However, I found out the Thursday before Christmas that I didn't make promotion from the supplemental board for my first promotion attempt. It took six months for them to tell me I wasn't worthy a third time (the first, I discussed during previous trips; the second, being passed over again on my second try; and this, time number three). I'm scheduled to be separated from the Air Force at the end of March—so, I won't have an opportunity to do any more riding in the spring.

PREPARATIONS ★

I've only begun to scratch the surface of preparing for life outside the military. I believed wholeheartedly that I would make the promotion at the supplemental board—so much so that I was in denial of the possibility that I could miss it. So, when I received the news, I was left in shock. If you've ever had your world rocked by something unexpected, you know the feeling. Logically, I knew not making rank was a possibility, but so much of life happens outside the world of logic, and my life is no exception.

I had to break the news to Glo, who seemed pretty numb already. She said that she had been preparing herself because she'd had a hunch it wouldn't work out the way I'd expected. I wish I had her insight. I still had to handle all of the preparation and begin a serious job search. Honestly, I had so much piled on my plate that I hadn't had any time to mentally process this mess. I was being pulled in five directions—and doing it all on my own, as Glo seemed paralyzed by life and could only sit and watch me do it all. So much happened in such a short time, it felt like I was suffocating and slipping on an ever-changing landscape, struggling to catch my breath and find my footing.

It'd been such a whirlwind of a mess that this trip of mine would actually give me space to process what was happening in my life for the first time, sans distractions.

Glo and I had taken a last trip with a group of our friends to Val Thorens, a popular French ski resort in the Alps. I thought spending some time among friends would help me digest and deal with what was happening in my life, but it, too, served only as a distraction—although a good and much-needed distraction.

I left work early so that I could pick up some supplies for my road trip. My boss granted me an extra day off the following day so that I could save my time off. He's a really good guy, and I know that my situation has really upset him. I wish he had been here when this mess began; he had the passion my former boss seemed to severely lack. Any time my promotion situation came up, my current boss would fall into a bad mood and tell me how aggravating the process is and how, if he could, he'd just keep me here. And, he didn't just talk the talk—he took every opportunity to push my situation up his leadership channels, looking for information and to make mention of the great job I had been doing, in spite of my situation. I was even the project officer for a four-star general's visit to our base, just so that my boss could put me out in front and showcase my abilities—then later, when the general was briefed about my situation, he would have a face and a positive experience to put to the brief. There was nothing the general could personally do about my situation, but my boss didn't

PREPARATIONS ★

care; he wanted to shout out his discontent from the mountaintops. This kind of support was in complete contrast to what I received earlier, when it really could have counted, and that added to the hurt I felt.

I made my first stop at a ski shop near my house to get some gear to keep me warm on the road. When the ski shop didn't have what I needed, I was forced to drive about 35 minutes to a sporting goods store. Luckily for me, it was past rush hour, so the trip was a smooth one. At the store, I walked up and down the aisles, looking for anything that would keep me warm on this upcoming ride. I knew it posed more risk—in terms of weather—than any other ride I'd done up to that point, but right then, I didn't care. I had a singular focus, and that was to complete my goal.

I filled my basket with a large pack of the "shake-activated" hand and toe warmers; a pack of multipurpose warmers that I could put on my thighs, stomach, or back if needed; a pair of glove inserts; and an extra set of thermal underwear. I imagined myself riding down the highway like a ball of fire with all the layering I intended to wear. I double-checked my basket to make sure I hadn't missed anything and made my way to the check-out counter.

While driving home from the store, I began making a list in my head of what I needed to do when I got home and in what order. It was already getting a little late in the evening, so I needed to finish my prep quickly and hit the bed. I stopped and grabbed some McDonald's on the way home for Glo and myself. (Glo had returned in September from her trip to take care of my Mom in California.) I ate en route to the house, mentally checking "dinner" off the list. When I got home, Glo was posted on the couch, glued to her laptop, as per usual. I set her food on the table in front of her and then grabbed my roll bag from the garage.

I was planning to be gone for only two days and a night, so I began packing accordingly. I packed a couple extra sets of underwear and grabbed four pairs of the thickest, wooliest socks I could find. I intended to double-up on just about everything. I tossed in some sleepwear and a spare set of thermal underwear. I planned on wearing two sets of thermal underwear for the ride, with a spare set in the bag so I could rotate them out on the return trip home. I also threw in a hoodie, just in case I needed some extra warmth. Although I had a pair of cold-weather riding gloves that were pretty warm, my friend James lent me his as a spare pair, because I wasn't sure what to expect. His hands are smaller than mine, so even though I could get them on, the fit was a little tight. I took them anyway; they'd be a back-up pair and most likely not needed.

PREPARATIONS ★

I packed my motorcycle vest filled with all the pins from my previous conquests. On the right side of the vest, I decided to sew on patches of the units I had served in up to my current assignment. I had a name patch sewn on from the HOG Chapter to which I belonged, the Maasland Chapter Belgium, based in Genk. Around my name patch, I placed all the pins I had collected, and on the back was a matching patch, larger and with the chapter name in gold lettering. I carefully folded my vest and placed it in the bag.

With all of the essentials in place, I put my journal, road map, and spare phone in the bag, zipped it up and lugged it to the garage. After securing my gear to the bike, I went back inside and laid out the gear I'd need for the morning: I was going to wear two sets of thermal underwear, two sets of wool socks, a T-shirt, and my textile jacket with the liner installed. (The jacket I wanted to wear—my 110th Anniversary leather—was out of commission because of a busted zipper.) With everything laid out, I went downstairs to chill with Glo before it was time for bed.

We didn't really talk much; I just watched TV while she played on her computer. She understood I needed to get away from the house to sort things out in my headspace. Our relationship had gotten progressively worse since she'd come back from California; it felt like a huge void of affection and love existed between us. We truly were simply roommates—sharing a space and trying to stay out of each other's way. I'd felt alone in this relationship for months now, and it didn't seem like things would get any better. After about 45 minutes of mindless television, I said my goodnights and went to bed.

As I drifted off to sleep, I cried. I felt miserable, trapped, suffocated, and alone. I fell asleep on the thought that if I didn't return from the trip tomorrow, life and the people in it would just push on, not minding one bit. I was depressed, and I needed to figure a way out of my spiral because Glo, Enwei, and Watson depended on it. I couldn't think here, so the road called and, eventually, sleep also came calling. I had a long ride ahead, and I planned to put the full weight of my anger, sadness, and pain on KB's two wheels. KB was my partner on the journey this weekend, and I took solace in knowing that he could handle every bit of it.

Chapter 15
HOME–WALES
27 JANUARY 2017

I woke up the next day in a much better mood than when I had gone to sleep the night before. The depressive and melancholic feelings had been replaced with a sense of adventure and excitement. I made a bowl of hot instant oatmeal and then took Watson out. My mind was steadied and focused that morning. After putting food in Watson's bowl, I made my way upstairs to get into my gear.

I had a lot of squeezing in to do, as I had packed on some serious weight since I passed my last fitness test back in October. I chalked it up to my stressful situation—and all of the eating out lately at our favorite restaurants. (We were trying to check off the good eateries at least one last time before heading back to the States.)

My weight didn't matter so much right then, so I pushed that thought aside and pulled on the second set of thermals. After putting on my boots, I pulled two balaclavas over my head and situated them in a way to keep my neck warm and prevent the cold wind from sneaking down the front of my jacket.

With everything on but my jacket, gloves, and helmet, I awkwardly walked back up the stairs to the bedroom. Glo was knocked out after pulling another long night sitting at her computer. Shuffling over to her side of the bed, I gazed at her sleeping face. She was beautiful. Her mouth was open a little; some drool dribbled onto her pillow. I had no idea how things were going to turn out for us—we were on a bad path, and I couldn't see a way out of it. I didn't want to lose her; I have so much love in my heart for her. But I knew that as things stood, I'd be miserable for the rest of my life.

I leaned over and gave her a kiss on her forehead; she stirred awake. She followed me downstairs, rubbing the sleep out of her eyes. She asked me a couple of questions about the trip as I pulled my jacket over my layered torso, punching my arms through the stiff sleeves. Once

HOME-WALES ★

I was all zipped up with gear in hand, she gave me a big hug—bigger than I'd had from her in a while—and wished me a safe trip. We exchanged "I love you's," and then I was out the door. It was time to ride; it was time to feel something other than miserable.

How crazy is it that in the dead of winter, facing separation from my career, troubles in my marriage, and uncertainty in life, I was sitting on KB, about to embark on a final European expedition? This was the most dangerous trip I'd taken on the bike so far, but with everything building up inside me, I needed a little danger in my life. The face of danger was as good as any at which to direct my ire.

I pulled the bike out in front of the garage and waited for the door to clink closed. While I waited, I put the garage door opener away in a zipper pocket, and put a set of hand warmers in my gloves. I had never used these before, but I figured that if they were good enough for skiers and snowboarders, they'd work for me. After activating the pouches, I put them on the backside of my knuckles, because that's where the cold wind would hit. I decided to hold off on the toe warmers for now; I wanted to test out my doubled-up wool sock method. With my gloves on and the warmers situated, it was time to roll. After a 10-minute ride to the highway, it was finally time to test my cold-weather fortitude (gained from spending time in Minot, Antarctica, and Svalbard).

It was already a chilly day, and it wasn't long before the wind chilled my fingers and toes. I rolled on, wriggling my fingers and toes, trying to keep the blood flowing to my extremities to keep warm. I *had* to figure this part out, because cold fingers and toes would make or break this entire trip. My core was staying warm because of the careful layering, so I could at least be thankful that I had only twenty little problems.

For the first couple of hours on the road, I couldn't think about anything other than keeping my twenty digits warm and comfortable. The cold kept my mind off the road, and before long I was stopping at a rest stop for gas, food, and coffee—and to warm up. I fueled up first and then rode to the parking in front of the restaurant. I shuffled, cold and hungry, to the food line inside.

After ordering my coffee and food, I sat down to relax a bit. While sipping the warm drink, I realized that this is the same rest stop that James, Michiel, and I stopped at on our day ride to the Belgian coast. I began to reminisce about how much fun we had. On a whim last year, the three of us decided to ride from my house to Ostend on the coast, with a stop for lunch in the city of Bruges. Michiel planned to make the six-hour round trip on his wife's sports bike. Meanwhile, James

HOME-WALES

intended to ride his starter bike, which was a 650-cc street bike. Needless to say, I was by far the most comfortable on that trip, but it was James's first trip, and he was stoked. We hit the coast and walked around the boardwalk, laughing and joking. Afterward, we rode to the medieval city of Bruges for lunch. I had made reservations at a restaurant that specialized in having a ridiculous selection of Belgian beers *and* cooking most of their dishes in beer—the name of the restaurant was Bierbrasserie Canibrus, and it was one of my absolute favorite places to eat.

We had to park far away from the restaurant because the city center of Bruges is a network of old and narrow one-way cobbled streets that makes it impossible to navigate—we ended up going the wrong way more than once down one-way roads. Eventually, we got to the restaurant after walking by the Belfry Tower (a medieval bell tower) and the Markt (Market Square) in the city center. Per usual, the food was incredible, and we ended up waddling out of the restaurant with overstuffed bellies. The uncomfortable full feeling made for a very long and arduous ride home, but I didn't feel it as much as the others did—overstuffed bellies on bikes not meant for long rides was a bad combination. They both survived the ride, only to reaffirm that they each planned to get Harley motorcycles so that they could actually enjoy rides. I swear, Harley should pay me as a traveling salesman.

After I finished my food and coffee, I decided to put the toe warmers to use; the initial ride was very educational, in a cold sense. While still seated at the table, I pulled a packet of toe warmers from my pocket and activated them. I took one boot off at a time and peeled the adhesive backing away from the warmer; at least I wouldn't have to worry about the warmers moving around in my boots. I carefully stuck each toe warmer underneath my toes and pulled my boots back on.

I gathered up my trash and tossed it as I made my way to the exit. I could already feel the toe warmers going to work. I felt good about my decision and was increasingly confident that the little warming pads would work wonders. I pulled my glove inserts on, followed by the hand warmers and the cold-weather gloves. I decided to flip the hand warmers over to the palm side for this stretch of road—the first experiment hadn't worked the way I thought it would. I thought that maybe on the palm, the heat from the activated warmer would radiate outward and reach my fingertips. At a minimum, it should warm my hands faster when I closed my fist.

Part of the fun of this trip was learning to ride in conditions completely different than what I'd encountered in the past. As much pain and cold that I endured, I loved it all—every minute of it. After adjusting the warmers in my gloves to allow for the most comfortable grip against the grips on my bike, I started KB up and pulled back onto the highway.

Back on the road, I could immediately feel the difference in warmth. Feeling encouraged by the positive change, I rolled back on the throttle and roared down the highway. It wasn't that my fingers weren't getting cold, but the warmer in my hand pressed against the bike grips, forcing the warmth deeper into my palm. This adjustment made it much easier to warm my fingers, and they stayed warm longer. My toes, however, warmed up and stayed that way; not even a hint of chill penetrated the warmth. I had placed the warmers on the bottom of the outer wool sock so the generated heat warmed up two layers of wool socks, essentially turning my boots into mini-ovens. While I still had to contend with preventing my fingers from getting chilled, solving the toes issue meant that a huge distraction had been lifted. Once I realized that I could battle the cold and win, I had a renewed sense of excitement and drive. Now the only thing that could possibly derail my ambition was if I were to hit snow and ice. Fingers crossed, it wouldn't come to that because I'm not so sure that I would be deterred.

I rode along, jamming to the music in my helmet, opting to clear my mind of the negatives in my life and instead focus on the present ride, my music as a current to carry my empty mind. I use music to float my consciousness so often, there should be a term for it. The music, combined with the road, has a similar effect on me as meditation.

With the French border looming ahead, I knew I was making excellent time. Crossing the border this close to the coast meant that before long, I would be at the train that would carry me and KB along the Chunnel. As with my previous rides, I felt a deep appreciation for the opportunity to ride around Europe as I pleased. I mean, how bad-ass was this—truly? Even with my life seemingly unraveling at the seams, I couldn't help but smile for the chance to enjoy this amazing life experience.

In a worst-case scenario, I would become broken, divorced, and destitute; yet no one could ever take away the fact that, in the dead of winter, I rode my bike across the United Kingdom. Money couldn't buy this experience. Sure, anyone with enough cash could buy a bike (not KB, though; he was meant just for me), and anyone could take time off work to plan a trip, but this trip in particular had other prerequisites. It required mental, physical, and spiritual fortitude to endure everything a person goes through on a long ride. Throw in some cold weather, and it adds a completely new dimension. Not everyone could handle this ride, and had I been in a different place in my life, perhaps maybe I couldn't, either. But, I wasn't in a different place in life. And as my mind flowed along the musical current of the road, for the time being I wouldn't want to be anywhere else in life. I hadn't even made it to the train before I began to feel the therapeutic and healing powers of this ride.

Finally, I made it to the train station. I rode through the ticket line, which was a lot cheaper than Trip Advisor advised it would be. I paid for my round-trip ticket for the train and then followed the lane all the way around a massive complex. Riding along the path, I saw what looked like a mall of sorts, or a giant rest stop. Too excited to get across the pond, I decided to skip all of that and go straight to the train.

I found my way to the line, parked the bike, and got up to stretch. The train came every 30 minutes, and I'd just missed the last one. It was still very early, so I wasn't watching the clock—yet. As I stretched, I looked around for a place to relieve myself; I really had to hit the head, and I wasn't going to be able to hold it much longer. I started to really regret not stopping off at that mall/rest stop I passed, when I thankfully spied a bathroom on the other side of the train entrance. Relieved, I did a weird jog with all of my gear on to get across several empty lanes to the opposite side of the waiting area. A piss never felt so good!

After washing my hands, I made my way back to KB and stood, stretching and kicking out the cramps. For being the end of January, and no longer on the highway with the wind hitting me in the body, the weather was certainly decent. The sun decided to come out for a visit, and though the temperature retained a slight chill, I was comfortable.

Finally, the train arrived. Everyone waiting in line got back into their cars and began to start their engines. We still had to wait for the inbound cars to offload, so I didn't rush to get back on the bike. Once all the cars had disembarked the train, the gate arm in front of the mass of vehicles rose, and I followed the cars into the belly of the train. The hold was pretty basic; not all that different than the ferry from Denmark to Germany, except this time I had to park my bike in the center of the train, not off to the side, and there were no straps to hold it in place.

After I settled the bike, I turned it off and took off some of my gear. After about 10 minutes, the train began to rumble and hiss, indicating it was about to leave. As we slowly pulled out of the station, I removed the hand warmers from my gloves and tossed them in the trash—they had a life span of only about five or six hours, and I didn't want to get caught riding when they decided to quit generating heat. I'd brought plenty of extras, so I wasn't concerned about conserving them. I pulled two new warmers out of my roll bag and set them on the seat, ready to activate them when we arrived on the other side. My toe warmers were designed to last longer than the hand warmers and were still good for quite a while, so I left them alone. With everything prepped, I leaned on my bike while the train gently bumped and swayed. There were no windows in the train car to see outside, not that looking at a concrete tube would be all that stimulating.

As the train dove under the English Channel, I let my mind wander back to my promotion situation. No matter how I tried, I just couldn't figure out how I ended up in this position. I mean, I checked all the boxes, I performed well, I kicked ass at my current assignment, and yet my peers were all being promoted over me. With a 92 percent promotion rate, I missed the cut—I felt extreme shame, hurt, and anger. I tried not to think ill of others who'd been promoted, but when I thought of some of those who had gotten promoted when I hadn't, it was hard not to feel resentful and envious. I knew people who'd been promoted to Major, having left their organizations in shambles—yet I built a winning and strong team from the bottom to the top, and I get the boot? Where is the fairness and justice of it all? What the hell?

I felt devastated, truly devastated. This was my career, the path to my ultimate dream—and in a blink of an eye, it was all gone. I had built back-up plans into my life, in the off chance that something like this might happen, but in reality I wasn't prepared to use any of them. I didn't want to—I wanted my military career. Besides, who would hire a failed Air Force officer? Sure, I had skills, but if I was unworthy for the Air Force, could I be worthy for any other organization?

To top it off, Glo has been struggling with this situation so hard, one would think she was losing *her* career! This is the first time I've gotten a chance to process it for myself because I've been so wrapped up in keeping her from spiraling (at which I'm also failing).

As my thoughts dove deeper into myself, the train swayed and rocked rhythmically from side to side. I wasn't ready to process this shit; at least not yet. I wanted to do this mental processing on the bike. As I pulled myself out of my spiral, I was left with a severe feeling of unpreparedness and anxiousness. I wasn't ready for what was to come after this ride, and I was terrified.

After roughly 30 minutes, the train pulled into the station on the other side of the Chunnel. I shook the negative thoughts from the forefront of my mind, got my gear on, and activated the new set of hand warmers. By the time the train doors opened, I was on the bike, engine running, and ready to roll. Upon exiting, I lifted my visor and deeply breathed in the English air. I exhaled quickly and pulled the visor down, coughing a little. This wasn't a movie! That was plain stupid—the air at a train station doesn't smell fresh at all.

Chuckling to myself, I followed the car in front of me clear of the exit ramp from the train car. I'd made it to England! I conjured a mental image of my travel list and penciled England into the 19th slot. Still following the car in front of me, I took notice of the signs posted everywhere reminding motorists to drive on the left side of the road. I was so incredibly nervous!

As I navigated the roads, I made sure a car was in front of me at all times until I made it to the highway. I've been to the U.K. many times, but this was the first time I've ever attempted to drive, and it felt so weird to be on the left side of the road. My focus remained razor sharp; I refused to get distracted by a stray thought for fear that I would fall into my automatic habits, all of which were geared to driving on the right side of the road.

The first roundabout I hit felt so unnatural, and it took a lot of concentration to intentionally curve toward the left. Finally, I made it to the highway, and I was able to relax a bit. Riding on the left-hand side of the road wasn't the only weirdness about the English traffic system—it took me quite a while before realizing that the distances and the speeds on the road signs were in miles, not kilometers. I was so used to seeing everything in kilometers in Europe that the change didn't register right away. I actually didn't realize it until I noticed that the speed reading on my GPS kept showing nonsensical numbers.

Once I figured out the change in speed, everything else fell into place. Suddenly the distances on the signs made sense as well. I had my GPS set up in kilometers, but since this was a short trip, I decided to just leave it in kilometers. No sense in changing it for a day-and-a-half. Armed with my new understanding, I made my way toward my first planned stop: Maidstone H-D.

The melancholic state of my life took a back seat, replaced by unbridled excitement. Today was going to be a big and fun-filled day, and Maidstone H-D was just the kick-off. It was no longer early in the morning, but to put things into perspective, I had already ridden through three countries (including crossing the English Channel), and many people were still lying comfortably in their beds, fighting the call to start their day.

Pretty soon, I was pulling off the highway en route to the dealership. I had adjusted to riding on the highway pretty quickly; I mean, the traffic only goes one way, but there were still differences. For one, the fast lane was now on the right-hand side of the road, and everywhere else I'd driven, it had been the designated slow lane. Once I finally wrapped my head around that craziness, I then had to contend with the fact that all the exits were on the left side of the highway. This realization wasn't as difficult to grasp, because many highways generally have at least a few left-hand exits—but to have so many was messing with my mind.

If riding on the highway took some adjusting, riding on city streets required a complete overhaul of my rider education! I decided to keep a car in front of me for a while, just until I acclimated to the driving etiquette—it was a completely different beast than riding on the highway, and my mind was firing on all cylinders. After some time, I began to understand the traffic flow and found it easier to conform to the traffic pattern. By the time I arrived at the dealership, I no longer required a "pace car" to show me the ropes.

Maidstone H-D was a very compact dealership. Shutting down KB, I stood up and stretched high. I hadn't really traveled all that far from the train, but being so hyper-focused on riding in a new environment—which seemed completely backward—was utterly exhausting. Upon entering the store, I had a flashback from my visit to the dealership in Hamburg, Germany. The people weren't all that friendly and largely ignored me, but I didn't care. First, I grabbed a steaming-hot cup of coffee. I wasn't in a rush, so I took my time walking around the store, looking at the merchandise.

I picked up a pin and a couple of poker chips, while sipping my drink; the poker chips were a newer collection item for me. For my birthday last year, Glo had bought me a Harley Davidson Poker Chip display case. Up until then, I hadn't given much thought to collecting these chips, and I had already passed on many places to collect from. She was very excited about the gift, and so was I—I had a new thing to collect and a new way to display all of my travels.

The first thing I did after receiving the display case was to create a list of all the countries I had visited and the Harley Davidson stores I'd been to. (There were a lot.) I began to call and go on online, looking for ways to get poker chips from all the places on poker-chip-to-get list. As the shops began sending me the chips, we watched the case slowly fill up, two at a time. (I decided to display two chips from each dealership so that I could show both the front and back of each chip.) Buying two of each may seem a little like cheating, but some of the chips had two legit sides, and I couldn't decide which side to show. When in doubt, put two out!

HOME–WALES ★

When I'd left for this trip, the display case was nearly full, and if things worked out as planned, I'd have only two empty spots remaining when this trip was complete. I'd even spent a Saturday riding around the Netherlands, hopping from one Harley Davidson shop to another in Amersfoort, Amsterdam, and Rotterdam, looking for pins for my vest and poker chips for my display. Not every Harley dealer carries their own poker chip, but enough of them did to make the weekend rides worth it, especially when the sun was out. I also started to buy an extra chip for James (he'd purchased a Harley Davidson bike, and was now just waiting for it to arrive)—he liked the poker chips also, so when I found some for myself, I'd get him one, too.

Once I finished my drink, I made my way toward the exit. I still had a lot planned to get through today. Before I reached the door, though, I noticed a custom Roadster on display. It was part of a "Battle of the Kings" contest around Europe, in which the majority of the European Harley dealerships partnered with a custom bike builder to craft a unique Harley motorcycle to enter the contest with. This custom-bike contest worked on a voting system. Therefore, to be really competitive, the sales reps and employees needed to heavily promote their store's bike above and beyond all the other entrants. This was a small location, so they probably struggled to get the same foot traffic that more popular locations received. I would've expected someone to approach me to get my vote, but no one did. The bike was beautiful; it was black laced with blood-red highlights. James, who loves the black-and-red color combination, would've drooled over this bike. I could've been convinced to spend my vote on this bike, but since no one seemed interested in promoting it, I withheld my vote.

Back at the bike, I packed up my purchases and got back into my gear. I needed to fuel up before hitting the highway again, so after loading up, I rolled back onto the road in search of a gas station; it took a while and a lot of riding on the surface streets until I found one. While gassing up, I contemplated the rest of my trip. I had stops in London, Reading, and possibly Oxford in England planned, before turning toward Cardiff, Wales, for the night. Looking at the time, hitting Oxford would be a tight squeeze, but if I got through London pretty quickly, I could probably make it.

Placing the nozzle back into the pump, I geared up and set the destination in my GPS to Warr's Harley-Davidson. This is the dealership I was most excited to hit—it's Europe's oldest Harley dealership, established in 1924, and it's right in the heart of London. I was excited to get some souvenirs from such a historic place, but I was also dreading riding around in the mess that is London traffic.

Back on the highway, I rolled back on the throttle, the excitement swelling in my belly. I was still dumbfounded that I was even on my bike at the end of January in England, heading to London. About an hour into the ride, I hit my exit toward the London streets and the London traffic. The traffic wasn't as bad as I thought it would be, but it still crept slowly along in some areas.

I was on the city streets for about another hour before arriving at the dealership. The store was in a commercial area, so there wasn't a lot of space. With the front of the store under construction, I rode around to the back. I found a fairly secure parking area and parked the bike in the gated lot. After taking off my gear, I made my way into the store.

This time, the staff were very friendly, greeting me as I entered the store. An associate walked me upstairs to the T-shirts, pins, patches, and poker chips, striking up a conversation along the way. I regaled the associate about my planned journey and the soon-to-be completed goal on the back of KB. She seemed pretty interested in my journey, but more so in the time of year I was making the trek.

After selecting the merchandise I wanted to buy, we made our way downstairs toward the register. We passed a display with a Warr's 90th Anniversary pin—and I *wanted* one. The anniversary was back in 2014, and the saleswoman said there were no more in stock—so I asked the obvious question, "Can I buy the one in the display?" She considered it for a moment and then went to talk to a manager. The manager came back with her, a small plastic baggy in his hand. As he handed the baggy to me, he told me that this pin was from his own personal stash. I was floored! Not only did they go out of their way to give me an old pin out of a private stash, they hadn't even charged me for it! They gifted me a limited-edition pin just because, and I was moved.

As we made our way to the register, she showed me *their* roadster for the "Battle of the Kings" competition. It was really dope. The first thing that came to mind was that it had a little bit of a steampunk vibe. The associate told me about how this store competed every year and that they had won many of the "battles." She also told me a bit about the custom builder that made the bike. Apparently, he was pretty well known in these parts and did a lot of work with the store. She asked if I had cast a vote for any of the other bikes along my trip, and I told her I hadn't, so she asked if I'd give it to their store. I gave it, and gave it freely. They had just demonstrated their commitment to me as a member

HOME–WALES

of the Harley Davidson family, so they had my vote many times over.

After paying for the merchandise, I walked around and took a couple of pictures with my phone. I even went out the front door to get one of the store front. I could feel time starting to drag on (it had taken me longer to get to the store than I anticipated), so once I finished taking pictures, I said my goodbyes and loaded up KB with my loot. Next stop: H-D in Reading.

It took me a very long time to get out of London proper. The traffic, construction, and whatnot just never seemed to end! I found myself just sitting on some streets for upwards of ten minutes without moving an inch, and when I thought I was catching a break, I'd get hit with new traffic from a different direction.

After about an hour and a half in traffic, I made it out of London. By this time, late afternoon–early evening was setting in, and I came to the realization that I'd be riding quite a ways in the dark. I decided to ax the Oxford leg, as it wasn't vital to the trip and I viewed it as being bonus anyway. Had I not been stuck in London for such a long time, I would've made the run; but as it was, I didn't want to be on the road in the dark any longer than necessary.

As I cruised on the highway, the chill in the air began to bite a little more. My gear was holding up nicely, however, so I had no need to change anything out just yet. Reading wasn't very far from London, but I made a stop prior to arriving to gas up. I considered getting some food as well, but with the sun racing toward the horizon, I told my stomach to wait it out—I didn't want to use up any more time than necessary.

After a quick fill-up, I was back on the road, focused on getting to the next stop as quickly as I could. By the time I made it to Reading, the sun was almost done setting. It was January, after all, so the days were shorter—it was getting dark outside, but it was still early in the evening.

I parked in front of the Reading Harley-Davidson shop and made my way inside. The staff were pretty quiet—more like Maidstone H-D than Warr's H-D—and they left me to my own designs. I found the pins and poker chips within minutes and was standing at the register to ring out. At the counter, I started chatting with the cashier, telling her about my travel goal. She seemed very disinterested, but for some reason I just kept talking. I mentioned that I wasn't sure if Wales would count toward my goal, since I wasn't sure if it was a country or a territory. For the first time since I began talking, she perked up. With no shortage of attitude, she replied, "Of *course* Wales is a country—why wouldn't it count?" It was obvious my ignorance struck a strong chord with her, so I explained that it was simply confusing for some of us who aren't familiar with the history and laws of the U.K. With that explanation, she switched back to her initial disinterested self, and completed my transaction. Whew—bullet dodged! I then went to grab a coffee and stretch out for a bit. Not wanting to sit around for too long, I gulped the coffee down and left the dealership.

Upon stepping out of the store, I saw that the sun had finally set and felt the air had taken on a lot more chill. The rest of this trip was to be made in the dark, which heightened my nerves but also gave me a sharper edge. Back on the highway, I rolled on the throttle and leaned into the ride with my remaining grit aimed toward my final stop for the night: Cardiff, Wales.

I kept my mind clear of anything but music as I scanned for anything and everything dangerous in the dark. Outside of Wales, I hit a lot of construction traffic, most of which was at a standstill. I split the lanes for a while, clearing the worst of it, but when rain started to fall, I fell into line with the rest of the vehicles. I had intended to continue splitting lanes, but I kept hitting those rumbles strips in the road meant to jar awake a sleepy driver. They were pretty large and mostly unavoidable, but with the rain falling, I began to fear that my tire could hit one at a weird and slippery angle, causing me to lose it. It was probably an irrational fear, but at the time my intention was to cross that border, bike intact.

It didn't take long for the traffic to subside, but as I came up to the Welsh border, the rain began to fall a lot harder. I preferred the rain to traffic, so I hunkered down and pressed on. I crossed a massive bridge, though it was too dark to see exactly what I was crossing.

Past the bridge, I took a quick second to celebrate—I'd done it! Wales was the 20th European country on the bike! What made this moment all the sweeter is that I was doing it despite all the uncertainty swirling in my life. Financially, this trip was inexpensive, although still probably ill-advised. But I had a strong need to complete this goal, to take this ride, and pay the cost. I was already starting to feel better in general, and though I knew I still had some issues to tackle while on this ride, for the time being, I just wanted to revel in my accomplishment.

By the time I made it to Cardiff, I was SOAKING wet. The rain hadn't stopped, or even slowed, since the border crossing, so the ride from the border to Cardiff was slow and steady. I rode around the city, reminiscing about the trip Glo and I had taken here a little more than a year ago. We had come to the U.K. to see the Detroit Lions (my favorite NFL team) play the Kansas City Chiefs. We went by train to Cardiff for the day, and I took her to the famous Dr. Who museum. It was a great trip, and although we didn't stay in town long, we both really enjoyed the vibe of this city.

Pulling into the parking lot of the hotel, I found a spot against the building, backed the bike in, and cut the engine. I wasted no time unstrapping my roll bag and unlocking and disconnecting my GPS. The rain was coming down hard as I clumsily worked at the clasps holding the bag to the luggage rack. Finally, I got everything off of the bike, locked the front forks, and made a beeline for the hotel lobby.

The reception area was relatively quiet; not too many people walking about. I trudged over to the front desk and plopped my gear down. I stood there, dripping, while the receptionist checked me in. I asked about security in the parking lot, concerned for my exposed bike, and she assured me that the bike should be safe. As she handed me my room key, I picked my gear up off the floor and apologized for the large standing puddle in the middle of the lobby floor. She chuckled and told me not to worry about it. I mentioned that the weather app on my phone hadn't said a thing about rain, to which she replied, "It always rains in Wales." Oh.

I dragged my stuff to the room and dropped it in the middle of the floor. Before stripping out of my gear, I ordered room service—a juicy burger, crispy fries, and a cold beer sounded right fantastic! With my order placed, I called Glo to let her know I'd arrived. While we chatted, I stripped off my gear and donned a robe provided by the hotel. I hung up my jacket and pants, hoping they would dry overnight.

The food arrived while I was still on the phone, and soon I was doing more scarfing than talking, so we said our goodnights and hung up. I couldn't tell you if the food was good or not because I devoured it, not stopping to savor any of it. With a belly full of food and beer, I took a scorching-hot shower to warm up my bones. It felt incredible, but not as incredible as the bed that was waiting for me. I hopped out of the shower, threw on my sleep clothes, stumbled over to the edge of the bed, and fell into the warm and inviting blankets. I was out cold before I landed, beyond wiped out from the day's adventures.

Chapter 16
WALES–HOME
28 JANUARY 2017

I woke up so incredibly sore! I looked at my phone, and it was still pretty early, so I let my head drop back to the pillow. I had no intentions of going back to sleep, but I wasn't ready to move my body just yet, either. My thoughts turned to the completion of my goal. I'd celebrated a little the day before, but right now I just wanted to bask in that elated feeling of crushing a goal.

As silly as it may sound, I was slightly afraid of not finishing this goal. I'd made a commitment to do it, and had I gone back to the U.S. without having completed the task, I would've felt the weight of another failure on my shoulders. My failure would've acted as an anchor, and I know it might just crop up later in life in the form of insecurity or self-doubt when I tried my hand at something new. That's the gamble I make when I commit to something I consider to be significant. It's why I bulldozed my way through my PhD program (despite numerous setbacks), my numerous travel goals, and the career goals that I set. I take it very hard when I fail to meet my personal commitments; that's why I can bask in the glow of completion, or spiral out of emotional control when I fail. It makes for a pretty crazy rollercoaster, and it's why I strive to achieve, not quit. At the moment my focus rested squarely on the completion of my goal; I could now say that hitting 20 European countries on the back of KB had been completed.

I rolled out of bed and stumble-walked to the bathroom. In no rush, I played on my phone before brushing my teeth and putting on deodorant. Still feeling sore and tired from yesterday's ride, I pulled out fresh clothes from my roll bag and slowly began to get dressed. That's when I realized that, in my exhaustive state, I'd completely forgotten to hang-dry some of my gear. Ughhh! This was going to be an uncomfortable return trip.

After taking an account of my "still wet" gear, it didn't turn out to be so bad. The wet gear was mostly my gloves and liners. I worked to dry the liners out with the hair dryer, and for the most part it worked. My gloves didn't fare as well as the liners, though. While trying to dry my gloves the same way I did with the liners, I popped a circuit breaker and the hair dryer abruptly stopped, the gloves still wet and clammy. I decided to try them out, maybe see if I could air-dry them while riding, assuming I could avoid any more rain. Worst-case scenario, I could wear James's pair of cold-weather gloves that I'd brought as a spare set. They were a little smaller, but if mine were a "no go," I wasn't going to have much of a choice. I finished gearing up and peeked out the window—it was overcast, and it looked as if more rain was on the weather menu for the day.

I lugged my gear downstairs and hit the check-out counter. While checking out, I asked the receptionist about the weather, and she replied, "It always rains in Wales." (Oh, right.) Chuckling at the creepiness of her reply (the exact same words as the other receptionist the night before), I took the receipt for the room and packed it in my bag.

After checking out, I made my way to breakfast for some quick eats and body fuel. The meal was a basic European-style continental breakfast, but it was still good. I used the time to stretch a little, making sure I didn't have any abnormal pains or aches. Other than severe soreness, all seemed to be in good working order.

Today's agenda had me riding all the way home by way of southern England. I sipped my coffee and mapped out my route on my phone. Today, the only two planned stops were Stonehenge (the famous prehistoric monument) and the Southampton H-D dealership. I was especially excited about the Stonehenge stop—I wanted to get a shot of Stonehenge with my bike front and center.

I finished up "brekkie" and made my way to my bike. When I stepped outside, I felt the rain. It wasn't raining hard, but it was going to be a pain to deal with; wet roads always are. I strapped everything down and wiped off my seat and controls with a rag as best I could. There were still streaks of water all over, but it would have to do. With a still-wet bike, I was off in search of a gas station—I was running dangerously low, but I hadn't had the energy to take care of it last night in the rain. Riding around the city center looking for gas brought back memories of the trip I took here with Glo. As I rode around reminiscing, I spotted a gas station and pulled in.

After filling up, I was on the road, making my way out of Cardiff. Ducking raindrops, I got to the highway, heading back the way I came the night prior. As I rolled away from Cardiff, the rain began to slow to a sprinkle until it stopped altogether. I rode across the massive bridge over the River Severn that I'd crossed the night before but couldn't see. It was wide and very large. The river below was beautiful, and I was sure that, on a bright, sunny day the area would make for a great place to get in some hiking.

As soon as I crossed the bridge back into England, the dark clouds receded back to the Welsh shorelines, and the sun came out in full force. The sudden change was drastic; crazy how even the weather respects man-made borders. With the sun out, the sky blue, and the roads dry, I cranked back on the throttle and let it roar!

Suddenly, the ride seemed like it would be alright after all. Wearing my wet gloves, I wanted to see if I could get them to air-dry, and though my hopes rose as the sun popped out of hiding, they were still very uncomfortable to wear, and quite distracting. Once I make it to the first stop, I'd have a good enough feel for needing to swap them out or not. But for the time being, I turned my attention to the beautiful countryside of sunny southern merry ol' England.

My first stop was Stonehenge—and I was beyond excited. I'd already been to the historic site about three years before and taken the tour. This time, I really just wanted to get a picture of my bike with Stonehenge in the background. I glided on the smooth roads for about two hours, through farming country and rolling hills. I hadn't really considered what southern England would look like, but turns out it's an amazing sight to behold—so I decided to keep my mind clear of the clutter for now; I didn't want to color the experience with intense and brooding thoughts.

My excitement reached a fever pitch as I pulled into the parking lot at Stonehenge. That's when I noticed that I couldn't *see* the monument. Previously, I had been able to see the stones from the parking area and the road, but now they were nowhere to be seen. A brand new visitors' center had been built, far away from the site! The surrounding roads were also closed off, so now the only way to see the historic site was to pay your entry fee, go inside the enclosed area, and hike to the site. There was no way to see the monuments from the road—so, no way to get that coveted picture. I felt bummed out; I was really looking forward to that picture. I parked KB and found an employee to ask if there was *any* way I could get the picture I was after; the answer was no.

I didn't want to waste the picturesque views, so I pulled the bike around to an empty parking lot area and snapped pictures of KB in front of the beautiful landscape. I even laid out my vest on the roll bag and shot some good angles, showing off my patches and pins. I was very disappointed, but I appreciated being here in the moment with my bike and the gorgeous weather. I decided to swap out my gloves with James'. The fit was tight, but they were much more comfortable than my wet gloves. With Stonehenge a bust, I turned my sights to the Southampton Harley-Davidson dealership, the last stop before turning homeward.

I rode on the back roads among the rolling hills, feeding off the sun and soaking in all of the beauty around me. I passed by Salisbury, the town with one of the few remaining and intact copies of the Magna Carta Libertatum (the famous Magna Carta document). On my first trip to London a few years ago, I came out to Salisbury because it was the location to catch the bus to Stonehenge. My buddy Eric and I had time to kill, so we walked around the town. We missed the viewing times to see the Magna Carta on display at the church. I was bummed—I had no idea something so cool resided in a seemingly random country-bumpkin town.

As I rolled through the peaceful countryside, I allowed myself to think about my work situation more, but not in a sad and depressive manner; rather, I turned contemplative. I began to piece together the decision points in my life and career that had led me to this point in time. I had been warned by a former squadron commander at my assignment in North Dakota that it'd be a mistake to take the posting in Belgium. He told me that the assignment "could" negatively impact my career because of how the position was viewed by the leadership within my career field. He warned that it would take a lot to keep up with my peers. Anything other than an outstanding and award-winning performance would put me behind the curve for promotion. I argued that I really wanted the Belgium assignment, and I remember thinking, "I'll crush this assignment! I'll put in some serious work and come out where I needed to be."

I held true to that, hitting the ground running. I took some lumps, big and small, but I volunteered for everything I could—even things I'd never done before. I mean, I sought to be bold and truly own my role as the operations flight commander.

New to the position in Belgium, I don't think my boss ever saw me as anything other than "green." I matured and grew, leaps and bounds, through my experience at this assignment. I led my team to win numerous high-level awards, recognition, and praise. I thought I was acing my role as flight commander and leader, yet I was repeatedly passed over—it just doesn't make sense!

I was proud of my performance, and I was crushed that the Air Force didn't feel the same. I became a better officer for the Air Force, and I felt like I was just being discarded. How was I less qualified to promote? I gave so much and transformed so much, just to be kicked to the curb. Damn it! How did it come to this? How can the Air Force tell me that I have nothing more to offer?

I could feel my eyes beginning to burn, the rush of frustration and anguish coming on full bore, hitting me in the chest like a bag of bricks. I hated that this was how things had turned out. I'd come to learn that a lot of people are a lot of talk—lip service—lacking the action to bring about change.

I'd never felt more abandoned than when I was told that most of the opportunities to volunteer for special projects would be given to one of my fellow flight commanders—who made Major on the same board which passed me over. These were the same volunteer opportunities that could've helped to add weight for my next promotion board meeting, yet they were giving them to a guy who'd already made it? What the hell? It made me feel like I was on my own, dangling in the wind, during this whole ordeal—as if my leadership truly felt I wasn't worth the effort.

Once I realized I was on my own, I put my nose to the grindstone and worked with what I had. I used every ounce of my network, determined not to lie down and die. With the help of friends and mentors, I crafted a package that I felt strongly about. But it didn't matter—I failed, again. I was passed over *again*, this time with a date for my release from the Air Force.

AAAAGGGGGHHHHH!!!!! I screamed into my helmet. Damn it! I had lost my career, everything I had worked for—vanished, just like that! I let more screams rip in my helmet until I was out of breath and the lower front half of my helmet was covered in warm spittle. Unbidden and furious tears streamed down my face as I screamed and cussed. I had removed the restraint, finally letting go of the calm façade I presented to everyone else.

My rawness roared in my helmet louder than KB's engine on the road. I couldn't even hear the music anymore, the current my mind was racing on now was pure rage. I knew I was in a tailspin, completely out of emotional control, and I didn't care.

At that moment, on a sunlit road in southern England, I cared only about feeling the rage I had managed to suppress for so long. Then suddenly, as if a switch had been flipped, I felt nothingness. I felt lighter; almost weightless—as if a massive weight had just been lifted from my shoulders. I felt . . . good? The music returned to my ears, and though I still felt the unfairness of my situation, for some reason I wasn't rage-filled anymore.

I started to wonder if I had mentally snapped and was now certifiably crazy. I chuckled in my helmet; I knew I hadn't snapped. I wasn't crazy—I'd just broken free of the shit that I'd decided to push down and not outwardly acknowledge. I had been carrying this crap inside for so long, and although I would still have to deal with the issues, I made the decision to no longer stuff it deep down inside. I faced a year's worth of emotion that had been bottled up; so, as with any fizzy drink after a good shaking, I popped my top. Feeling astonishingly better, I decided to return my focus on the ride, the music, and the beauty of the day.

Cruising along and feeling renewed, I soon made it to Southampton, England; the town serves as a port on the English Channel. The air smelled keenly of saltwater; a smell I enjoy. I rode on toward the Southampton H-D dealership, parked the bike at the shop, and removed my helmet and gloves. After a big and healthy stretch, I made my way inside.

The dealership was compact and very busy with a lot of people milling about. Making my way inside, I wandered around with the masses, looking at the bikes on display and the merchandise for sale. I had trouble locating the items I enjoyed collecting, so I found someone to ask about the pins and poker chips; a saleswoman pointed them out.

As I picked out a pin and some poker chips, she and I got to talking about her tattoos. She had some amazing work; unfinished, but the line work was crisp. She told me about her artist, and I shared that my wife and I had had some tattoo work done in London, so we compared notes about the two shops. I paid for my merchandise and then turned my attention to the next priority—my stomach. I was so hungry I could have eaten anything.

I packed away the items I'd purchased as well as the rain cover for the roll bag. (I no longer needed it as the day was just so bright and blue.) I mounted KB and made my way to a McDonald's across the highway. Because this was the last planned stop, I was officially on the homestretch at this point—I felt good and ready to make the trek home. I ordered my usual two-cheeseburger combination meal and grabbed a table at the window so that I could see my bike in the parking lot. I chose to stand while I ate so that I could give my tailbone a break, incorporating little stretch actions while I ate. After my meal I hopped back on the bike and rode to the gas station next door. After a quick fill-up, I was back on my grind, headed to the train station in Dover, England.

I let my mind slip into my music for this leg of the trip, choosing to bask in the sunshine and good vibes pumping from my speakers. Traffic picked up somewhat along the way, but the two-and-a-half hours passed by pretty quickly. I made a stop to fuel up about 20 minutes outside Dover. I decided to forego coffee this time, but I did pop a couple of Fisherman's Friend mints for an extra kick in the pants. I didn't dally at the gas

WALES-HOME

station, either, because I wanted to try to catch the next train back across the Chunnel.

As I pulled up to the ticket booth and showed my passport and return ticket, I felt a sense of pride and excitement. I was about to cross the English Channel, headed home, having accomplished an amazing feat. I guess I wasn't done fully celebrating, and I was okay with that.

The wait for the train wasn't as long as the day before, and soon I was pulling into the train. I situated the bike similarly as I did for the trip over and removed some of my gear. I decided to replace my hand and toe warmers while on the train. My hands were sore from the warmers being crammed between my palms and the grips, so I stretched and massaged them, working out the soreness the best I could. There was nothing I could really do about the tight fit; the alternative would leave me with frozen mitts. As the train bumped and swayed underneath the English Channel, I began stretching my entire body. I was on the verge of completing this trip, and this last part was going to feel like the longest stretch of road.

As the vehicles poured out of the train at the French station, I could see the sun starting to dip pretty low in the sky. It was getting dark, and rather quickly. I wanted to cover as much ground as possible heading home before nightfall set in. With newly replaced warmers in my gloves and boots, I was ready to rock 'n' roll for the homestretch.

I hit the road like a madman, initially nervous that I would have forgotten how to ride on the right side of the road—but it didn't take long for me to slip back into my old right-sided habits. With the music cranked, I hunkered down and rolled on the throttle. I had no fear of getting flashed by the speed cameras, because by the time the tickets made it to my job through the mail, I'd be long gone, back to the States. Without that constraint, I blazed through northern France.

I crossed the Belgium border just before nightfall, so the rest of the ride would be in darkness, but I knew I could handle it. The longer I was on the road and the closer I got to home, the more anxious and excited I became. And, the closer I got home, the closer I was to completing another grand adventure. I'm not sure why I enjoy adventuring so much, but I do know that nothing gets me going more than planning and then finishing an adventure.

I stopped one final time between Ghent and Brussels to fill the tank and put a little food in my belly. After I gassed up KB, I pulled up to the front of the restaurant so that I could eat and keep an eye on the bike. I went through the food line, selecting everything that was warm, and topping it off with a piping-hot cup of coffee. I found a tall table by the front window and again stood while I ate, stretching my glutes.

I was getting more sore—and faster, at that. On the road, I'd developed a set of motions and movements that helped me stretch in a limited-capacity sort of way. But while I ate, I was able to get in a deeper stretch, and I'm sure I looked all the weirder for my routine. When I finished my meal, I put my dishes away and got in one final, big stretch. Before I knew it, I was on the final leg of the trip! No more stops for gas, food, or breaks. I cranked my music, fell into my tunes, leaned my head forward behind the windshield, and rolled on the throttle. It was nighttime, with very little traffic, and I was ready to be home. I call that a recipe for some serious speed!

Before long, I was pulling off of the highway at the exit toward the house. I was on home turf now, and it felt great! I relaxed and enjoyed the 10-minute ride to the house. As I pulled into my driveway, I had a final sense of completion—I'd made it home!

I pulled the bike into the garage and after two final revs, I shut KB down. I sat on the bike for a little bit, soaking in the good feeling and lamenting that the next time I cranked KB up, it would be to take him to the dealership to get prepared for shipping stateside.

★ TWO WHEELS DOWN

I savored my final excursion across Europe for about a minute longer, and then it was time to come back down to earth. And while I felt lighter for having released much of my pent-up rage earlier, it didn't mean I'd escaped from my reality. Wearily, I pulled my bag off of my bike and headed to the front door, closing the garage door behind me.

Each step toward the front door weighed heavier with the reality of my predicament, severely blunting my excitement for having closed out a major goal and milestone. I was finally home, no longer on the road, and it was time to face my life going forward. The door opened, and I was greeted by Glo and Watson—I was being greeted by my life.

EPILOGUE

Countries Traveled:

- ~~Belgium~~
- ~~The Netherlands~~
- ~~Germany~~
- ~~Denmark~~
- ~~Sweden~~
- ~~Austria~~
- ~~Liechtenstein~~
- ~~Switzerland~~
- ~~Poland~~
- ~~Czech Republic~~
- ~~Slovakia~~
- ~~Hungary~~
- ~~Slovenia~~
- ~~Croatia~~
- ~~Italy~~
- ~~San Marino~~
- ~~France~~
- ~~Luxembourg~~
- ~~England~~
- ~~Wales~~

Total Miles/Kilometers Traveled: 5,664 mi/9,115 km

EPILOGUE
LIFE AFTER THE RIDES

First, I'd like to thank you for riding along with me on this journey. There were a lot of highs and lows throughout the four trips to these 20 countries, but you decided that my story was worth following to the finish. For that, I am truly grateful.

The following section is meant to provide you with a bit of closure to some of the big rocks that I dealt with over the course of my rides. As I stated in the foreword, this is about real life, affecting real people—this was not going to be fiction. I also suggested at the outset that you shed certain expectations—including a happy ending at the end of the story—so that you may experience real life with me. And you experienced with me—especially on the last ride—that life came to a boiling point on multiple fronts. A lot has changed since that final ride, and if you're interested, read further to see where things stand as of the writing of this book. You may be surprised at the turn of events; I know I was. . . .

MARRIAGE

What to say about marriage? It's easily the hardest and most dangerous adventure on which I've embarked; no kidding. By no means are Glo and I fully healed from past hurts and the effects of my transition out of the military, but we've reached a new height in our love and respect for one another. We still struggle, as does any couple, and while we continue to transition, there are certain realities that we've both had to confront, some easier than others.

During the transition, we both struggled with the idea of going our separate ways. We had multiple raw and honest conversations on the topic of divorce. I was certain we were going to split for good, and the thought hurt greater than any pain I've known. There is a reality in which I know that we could be happier apart than we are together, but that is only one reality in a sea of others. What we've decided is that whatever we have to face, we will do so together. At times, this

EPILOGUE ★

may be to our detriment—both individually and as a family—but together we are committed to face whatever may come.

I'd love to be able to write that I braved the down times out of true love, but I promised truth and no fiction, right? The truth of it is, in the times when I felt that logically we'd be better off going our separate ways, I also felt an overwhelmingly strong and intense fear of letting someone go whom I still loved dearly. I felt an intense fear of being alone, playing the "What if?" games in my head.

I admit there were times in which I stayed in our relationship out of cowardice, not love. I've never stopped loving my wife, and thank God for our conjoined love because I wouldn't want to spend the rest of my life with anyone else. But, I can honestly say that fear did drive my decision-making during parts of our relationship.

Glo and I are at a point in our relationship where we are working on rediscovering what we want to be for one another. It's a long and arduous road, but not an impossible one. It will require growth and maturity on both our parts, but once we reach the point in our marriage in which we understand who we are for one another, I have no doubt that we will make a most powerful couple. I look forward to that day, and I truly believe in my heart of hearts that that day is ahead of us. I expect it to take time to reach that day, and even once we've reached it, there will be times in which we regress. But, once we achieve that power as a couple, I believe we will work to maintain it out of love for each other.

We put some of our plans on hold while we waited for the Air Force's decision on my reinstatement to active-duty service. But, we remained secure in our willingness, desire, and love for one another to navigate the impact of the impending results together, no matter the outcome.

JOB AND TRANSITION

If you've never gone through a forced mid-life crisis, I can tell you it is intense! We flew from Belgium to the U.S. east coast while we waited for our car to come into the Baltimore port. Car shipping takes anywhere from four to eight weeks, so I had to rent a car to haul us around the country. We both had family in the Maryland area, so we bounced around from hotel to motel for almost two months there, visiting and job hunting.

I furiously sought to get back in the military as a reservist or in the Air National Guard. I sought out Remotely Piloted Aircraft (RPA) pilot opportunities, as it was a career field hurting for pilots something fierce. I connected with Nicholas, a Guardsman, who took me under his wing, not only introducing me to his network of contacts but also providing some much needed mentorship and guidance, both professionally and personally. He had gone through a similar situation when he was on active duty, so he could relate to what I was experiencing. And he used his experience to help me understand my situation for what it truly was—a new start.

I put together three different packages to be an RPA pilot, and one by one, I was rejected. After each rejection, I would ask for feedback so that I could make my next package for the next unit even stronger. Time and again, I received the same response: "Your package is pretty strong, and we can see that there is no negative information on you, but we just don't want to assume the risk of taking on a twice-passed-over Captain." Each time I heard that, I cringed; so much was out of my control, and it was infuriating. I understood their position, but I also understood my value and just wanted a chance to prove it. Eventually, it became clear that the RPA community wasn't interested in me. And because I had invested so much time preparing these packages to pursue a new career as an RPA pilot, it was time I hadn't been looking elsewhere for opportunities.

I began reaching out to friends of mine in the Reserves, looking for something I could latch onto.

Finally, a work and travel friend of mine, Mike, linked me to his Reserve unit at Vandenberg Air Force Base in California.

After the powers that be reviewed my package and interviewed me, they agreed to take me on. I was so excited to tell Glo—the new posting would take us to California, a place she wanted to be.

As we were prepping for the move cross-country, I began to look for civilian work in California. Now that I'd found a unit to take me, I had to submit a waiver to the Air Force requesting entry into the Reserves, because it's not usually allowed, given my situation.

The waiver process can take up to six months or more, so in the meantime, I gathered Glo and the animals, and we drove the rental car cross-country toward California. We stopped along the way to see her brother and his family, visited the Grand Canyon, and (of course) hit multiple Harley Davidson dealerships en route to Riverside, California. My mom and her husband, Darryl, had agreed to let us stay with them for a couple of weeks while we figured some things out.

On the day we arrived in California, I received a call that my car had finally arrived at the port in Baltimore. Putting aside the fact that I'd need to go pick it up and drive cross-country again, it was nice to finally have arrived at a place to call home, for now.

EPILOGUE ★

After a visit to the Reserve unit, I was excited to get started, but I still had to navigate the waiver process. We stayed with my mom while I looked for work. About two weeks after we arrived, I got a ping on the job front. I had been recruited by an executive recruiter from Target (the chain store) to be an operations manager at one of their distribution centers. I ran through the entire process; they made me a job offer—within my requested salary range—and I accepted. I was so excited!

Finally, life was beginning to gain some traction. It might not have been what I'd wanted, ideally, but we were going to make the most of this situation and wait for a full-time opening with the Reserve unit. I still needed to fly back to Baltimore to pick up our car; it had arrived stateside the day we pulled into Riverside, about three weeks prior. With a new job locked in, a Reserve unit fighting for me, and a refreshed outlook on our new life, I made my way to Baltimore.

When I arrived in Baltimore, I stayed the night with my brother-in-law, Edgar, and his wife, Margie. This guy is crazy talented, and fiery about transforming his art into something the masses can enjoy. The three of us had a great night of discussion and laughter. The next morning, on his way into work, he took me to get my car from the port.

I didn't have to wait very long before I laid eyes on my Maxima. I did my checks on the car, making sure there was no more damage to the vehicle than when I dropped it off, and signed for receipt. After a quick fill-up, I made my way to Andrews Air Force Base to meet up with a friend for lunch, my Air National Guard mentor, Nicholas. I caught him up on everything that had transpired, thanked him for all of his mentorship and guidance, and made sure he knew how much of a positive difference it had made in my life.

After lunch, I made my way to my Dad's house, my last stay before I hit the road back to California early the next morning. I had a chance to hang out with my dad, stepmom, and two little sisters for the night. There was a lot of excitement because one of my sisters was graduating from high school and prepping for college in the fall. I was proud of all her hard work and was excited to see her excel. Next year, my youngest sister would be in the same position, and I was just as excited for her.

In the morning, my dad and I had breakfast together before I hit the road. My dad is a special guy—he has a huge heart and cares so much about his family. He always ensures his family is taken care of, and he helps in every way he can think of. He is one of the most generous people I know, a characteristic I strive to emulate.

EPILOGUE

He expressed his frustration about my situation and also his pride in my ability to adapt and overcome.

I hit the road shortly after we parted ways, making my way back across the country to California. At my first stop for fuel, I received an email out of the blue that I hadn't expected. It was an email from the Air Force Personnel Center, and attached was the results of the supplemental board that met back in January. This was the absolute last chance that I could promote and get back on track with the active-duty life I had envisioned all those years prior.

I started to open it and then hesitated. What would I do if I hadn't made it? What would I do if I *had*? The chances of making Major on this board were so slim that I had already resigned myself to being passed over a fourth time. But that resignation didn't stop my heart from thumping out of my chest. The hesitation didn't last long—I opened the attachment to read my fate. "Congratulations on your selection for promotion. . . ."

Tears streamed down my cheeks as I sat in the car. I read that first line over and over again. I couldn't believe it—I'd made it! I thought, This changes everything—or does it? All of a sudden I couldn't think straight; I was so taken aback by this that I just sat, frozen in shock.

Slowly, I began to come back to reality. I connected my phone to the Bluetooth in the car and pulled out of the gas station. First person I called—Glo, of course! While on the road that day, I called everyone I could think of to tell them the news. The feeling was an unbelievable sense of relief and weightlessness. I felt as if I had been walking around with a 400-pound-weight jacket since finding out that I had been passed over, and with just the first sentence from this last decision, I had finally shed that ridiculous weight.

I won't go into detail about the trip back to California; suffice it to say, it was an extraordinarily happy trip. After talking it over with Glo, we decided to go back to Active Duty. I let the Reserve unit know about my decision and thanked them for giving me an opportunity when no one else would. And with four days before I was to start my civilian job, I also called my recruiter at Target, explained the situation, and thanked them for their consideration.

After a nine-month wait, the reinstatement process was completed, and we received our orders to the beautiful state of Montana. I was in a position to pass on the wisdom and kindness that I experienced on my journey to the up-and-coming officers who would one day take my place. Glo and I are so happy and relieved. It has taken a while, but we have finally fallen back into a good life rhythm. My promotion ordeal has given me a new appreciation for my opportunities to create positive

EPILOGUE

change, big and small, opportunities that I will not be taking for granted again.

LIFE

Life has a funny way of working out, doesn't it? Had you told me in January of 2015—when I was still waiting for the very first promotion results—that I'd be going through what I went through, I'd have laughed in your face. Completely unthinkable! And yet, here we are.

While we waited for the reinstatement process to run its course, I kept active. I constantly searched for ways to grow and be productive. In fact, this very book is one product of that search. Glo and I attended a couple of Landmark Forum courses, which really helped us learn to identify areas in our lives in which we could take back control, and to create new possibilities for ourselves as individuals and for our marriage.

I had just started a Green Belt process improvement certification before my Belgium separation. This is a continuous process improvement method that is used to not only solve organizational problems but also create processes to sustain the fixes. My mentor kept me engaged so that I could finally finish the project and receive my certification.

I also searched for writing courses, Spanish courses, and more. Coincidentally, I found a gallery/coffee shop in which to hang some of my travel photography for sale. This Californian coffee shop, the Daily Brew, reminded me of the coffee shop called the Broadway Bean and Bagel Co. in Minot, North Dakota, which was where I first sold some of my work. Both have a very laid-back feel, and I've called each one my second home at different points in my life. I've even launched a travel-photography website on which to display and sell photographs I've taken from all over the world.

I hold no anger or resentment toward the Air Force or any of my former supervisors, as I know that life just happens. While some would point to the flaws in the promotion system, I would point to the amazingness of the people. So many people reached up and supported us during our transition—family, friends, coworkers, and complete strangers all pitched in to make my experience one of love and kindness rather than resentfulness and anger. There is much that I would've missed out on had I not gone through this ordeal, and I've grown to appreciate the opportunities gained since.

I've spent more time with my mom than I had as a child, and we are closer than ever. I deeply admire her passion and her grind; she works tirelessly for the benefit of others. I've adapted her deep, critical thinking and analytical skills to much of my life, and I have only benefitted. I grew up watching her fight for her goals,

EPILOGUE

working her fingers to the bone in order to not only provide but also achieve. And for that, I admire her greatly.

I have decided to live as best I can, through and in between all of the obstacles. I have a new appreciation for what life actually means to me. Life is a series of events that happens when it happens, regardless of plans or intentions. Accepting what is and is not gives you the power to create in your life what could be, regardless of the roadblocks in your path. Don't live life waiting for the other shoe to drop; instead, live life fully between the footsteps—that's where the adventure awaits!

Thanks for joining me on one hell of a ride!

—C.R. Boney

ABOUT THE AUTHOR

I am a USA-based writer of creative non-fiction and fiction. This is my first foray into non-academia focused writing, though my publishing credits include *Crossing the Military Rank Divide: A Qualitative Study of Military Leadership and Motivation in the USAF*. I am currently in the US Air Force, though I spent my formative years between living in Detroit, MI and San Antonio, TX.

I undertook the writing of this book after hitting a downturn in my military career. After being discharged from the service for failure to make promotion, I turned to my passion for writing while I waited on resolution for an appeal to the decision. I am an avid traveler and keep travel journals detailing each of my adventures.

The four trips detailed in this book are pulled from actual journal entries made during the time of my travel.

I am passionate about bringing stories to life, giving the reader relatable characters with whom to endure the struggles and celebrate the victories. When I decide to retire from the military life, I seek to become a full-time writer, sharing the crazy adventures that have been my life and the fictional life of the characters rattling around in my head.

Printed in Great Britain
by Amazon